YAS

ALLEN COUNTY PUBLIC LIBRARY

**FRIENDS
OF ACPL**

 W9-BBG-862

John Bunyan

Author of The Pilgrim's Progress

Sam Wellman

CHELSEA HOUSE PUBLISHERS
Philadelphia

Cover Design: Brian Wible

First published in hardback edition © 1999 by
Chelsea House Publishers, a division of Main
Line Book Co. Printed and bound in the United
States of America.

© MCMXCVI by Sam Wellman. Original paperback edition
published by Barbour Publishing, Inc.

1 3 5 7 9 8 6 4 2

The Chelsea House Publishers World Wide Web site
address is http:\\www.chelseahouse.com

Library of Congress Cataloging-in-Publication Data

Wellman, Sam.
    John Bunyan / Sam Wellman.
    p.   cm. —(Heroes of the faith)
    Includes index.
    Summary: Describes the life of John Bunyan, itinerant English
    Puritan preacher and author of many religious books and sermons,
    including "Pilgrim's Progress."
    ISBN 0-7910-5035-1 (hc.)
    1. Bunyan, John, 1628-1688—Biography—Juvenile literature.
    2. Authors, English—Early modern,1500-1700—Biography—Juvenile
    literature.   3. Puritans—England—Biography—Juvenile literature.
    [1. Bunyan, John, 1628-1688. 2. Authors, English. 3. Puritans.
    4. Great Britain—History—Puritan Revolution, 1642-1660.]
    I. Title. II. Series: Heroes of the faith (Chelsea House Publishers)
    PR3331.W45   1998
    823'.407—dc21   98-19852
    [b]   CIP
                                                                   AC

John
Bunyan

In fond memory of Jerry Wellman:

Now, now look how the holy pilgrims ride,
Clouds are their chariots, angels are their guide. . .

one

A Foolish Adventure

John Bunyan and his band of merry men crept along the south bank of the River Ouse. Their village of Elstow was now below the horizon far to the southeast. And so was the farm near Kempston where they had stolen apples. The sun was strong enough to make John squint.

"We'll stop right here, men!" he snapped to the two boys who followed him. "Fall out!" John plopped down and crunched an apple in his teeth. He was immediately lost in thought. If only they could find wild honey. They could ferment it into bee wine. There was so much mischief he wanted to do.

"Why do we always play Robin Hood and his merry men, John?" asked a boy who remained standing. He was named John too, but was known to the other two only by his last name: Rogers.

"Don't you like the apples we steal from the rich and give to ourselves, the poorest wretches we know, Rogers?" snickered Harry, relaxing on the ground next to John, and eating an apple too.

"Why don't we play soldier?" questioned Rogers. "We'll soon be in a great war. . . ."

"Oh yes," mocked Harry, "we lads of Bedfordshire must be ready to fight for his majesty King Charles and England in this momentous year of 1642." The sarcasm left his voice as he warmed to the subject, "I don't believe there will be a war. This talk of soldiers moving about the countryside is just the idle talk of the gentry at the village green. Besides, if there is a war, my step-father says the men in Bedfordshire will fight for the Parliament. Never again will the king dismiss our good men of Parliament for ten years as King Charles has done."

"Parliament! Those traitorous rebels!" barked John Bunyan, suddenly aware of the conversation. "We'll have their heads!" John believed there was going to be a war. And he would have loved to play a soldier for the king, but how could he steal apples if he played soldier?

"If you're so brave, John," sneered Harry, pointing farther along the path beside the river, "why don't you have the head of that snake?" Harry was always difficult. And his mouth dirtied the air with profanities, just as John's did. John never noticed them though unless Harry was particularly difficult, as he was now.

"There aren't any snakes out in October, Harry," scoffed John, but when he looked up the path he saw Harry was right. "It's sunning itself," John whispered in explanation. He studied it hard. The snake was deathly gray with grim black diamonds shrouding its back. In a triangular head glowed amber eyes, slashed by vertical slits as black as doom. Its belly bulged gruesomely, as if it had eaten some plump field mouse. The snake was probably sluggish. Yet the black tongue slithered in and out in a snaky rhythm.

John silently motioned the others to stay back. No one protested. He crept to the edge of the river and found a long, thick branch that had floated against the reeds. He gently picked it up and fingered it for cracks. It was solid. He tiptoed toward the snake, making sure his shadow never crossed the fat serpent. Clutching the branch with

8

both hands he raised it over his head. Then he smashed the fat body just behind the head.

"You got it!" screamed Rogers. The snake writhed, its back broken. It was unable to crawl. Its jaws ratcheted sideways in agony.

"It's an adder," said John calmly. "One bite from that cruel, lipless mouth, Harry, and you would swell into a purple toad and die."

"It isn't poisonous at all," disagreed Harry. "It's nothing but a common old water snake."

"One way you can prove that," suggested John, "is to open its mouth and look at its teeth."

Harry backed away. "I don't have to prove anything."

"Then I suspect that I do," said John. He grabbed the snake behind the head and wedged a stick between its jaws. He found a second stick to lower its two long fangs. "See."

Harry grunted, as if not convinced. But he wouldn't come any closer to look.

"I'll hand you one," said John. And he proceeded to extract a fang with his fingers. It was the sort of dangerous thing he did all the time. It was the reason he was the leader of these boys. He was tall and strongly built, and clever as a fox, but those were not the reasons they followed him. It was his unrelenting fearlessness. John was afraid of nothing. And he was the first to admit it had nothing to do with God or the Bible the pastor at Elstow Church tried to shove down his throat. John's courage came from within himself.

He held out his hand. In his palm poison bubbled out of the end of the fang. "Take it, Harry—or admit I'm right."

Harry's eyes were wide. "Y—y—you're right," he stammered.

Rogers pointed to the west. "Something peculiar is

happening up there where the river widens in the flats."

John peered upstream as he washed the poison off his hand in the river. Dust was hovering north of the river as if some shepherd was driving sheep toward the river.

"Let's go see, men," he said.

They crept through the willow trees and underbrush along the river. After a while they knew that the dust was caused by men. Hundreds of men. As they marched to the river they raised dust from fields freshly plowed and sown with winter wheat.

Rogers whispered, "They're wading the sandy flats of the river and marching on to the south. They must be in a hurry not to cross the river on the bridges at Olney or Bedford."

"That's not the reason," snapped John. "They are avoiding the bridges. They mustn't be seen. They're the king's men. I see one carrying the royal standards."

"You're right," agreed Harry. "And look at the pikemen with their shiny helmets."

High over the marching men sharp pikes also gleamed in the bright sun. And marching among the pikemen were men in large floppy hats with plumes. They carried muskets on their shoulders. They were the musketeers. Swords girded to the sides of all the marching soldiers clacked against one another. Watching them closely were a few men on foot, wearing hats with even larger plumes and ornate gloves to their elbows, carrying neither pike nor musket. They must have been the officers of the foot soldiers.

"Look," whispered Rogers. On the north side of the river, dust swirled around dozens of men on horses. They wore plumed hats and long boots. "A troop of cavaliers is coming to cross the river too. They might spot us."

"Why should we care if the cavalry sees us?" protested

John. "Don't we serve King Charles?" And he stood up in plain sight. Almost immediately one of the cavaliers bolted his horse across the flats of the river onto the bank and stormed toward the boys, with saber drawn.

"Let's go!" yelled Rogers.

"Stay put, friend. Let me handle this," said John. He was not the least concerned. He well knew he had a face for all occasions, wide-mouthed and brown-eyed. When his mouth did not turn down in a leer and his eyes burn with devilry for his loyal followers, his face could be as placid as a cow's.

In a cloud of dust the cavalier brought his gray warhorse to a thunderous stop in front of them. His drawn saber flashed in the sun. A long scabbard hung from his broad leather belt. Two pistols were tucked in the belt. His dark brown hat flaunted a blue plume. His suit was tan velvet trimmed in blue. He wore huge boots of dark brown suede. Over his shoulder fluttered an elegant cape of blue satin. "Who are you?" he demanded. "And where are you from?"

John bowed. "We're lads from the town of Bedford of the shire of Bedford, good sire," he answered, putting on his most placid face, "and more than willing to serve His Majesty King Charles."

"Ha!" scoffed the cavalier. "Do you think he needs common trash like you Roundheads?"

"What does Roundhead mean, sire?" asked John pleasantly, though feeling pinpricks of anger.

The cavalier's saber deftly impaled John's hat and flipped it off his head. "I mean the round sandbur of a head you hide under your pointy hat, boy." Not one red hair on John's head was much longer than an eyelash. The cavalier scowled. "Don't you see how a real gentleman wears his hair?" The cavalier's thick hair came to his shoulders in

11

glistening ringlets.

The cavalier was young, no more than about twenty. Anger boiled in John now. It was too embarrassing to explain his father sheared his hair so it couldn't harbor lice. But John's anger surpassed quibbling over hair. For a long time he had wanted to fight for the king. It had occurred to him in dark moments the Royalists might think he was unworthy. After all, he was nothing but the son of a tinker. But now that he saw it was really true, he seethed with resentment. The betrayal dissolved his placid mask. "Let's go," he grumbled to the other boys.

"You saw nothing at the flats," said the cavalier. "Do you understand me, Roundhead?" He was talking to John only, as if the other boys needed no persuasion. "No one in Bedfordshire must know the king's troops are moving south."

"I see nothing but pea-brained sheep crossing the river," snapped John.

"That's a good boy. . . ." Suddenly the cavalier's face was angry as he studied John. "You mean that another way, don't you, you insolent dog?"

Suddenly the cavalier pulled a quirt and lashed John across the shoulder. He jumped down from his horse, grabbed John's arm and beat him with the quirt. John wanted to scream, "No, I'm only thirteen," but he would not beg for mercy. And the cavalier wouldn't stop beating him. The stinging from the quirt passed into a fearful numbness that smelled of dust and death. . . .

two

A Daring Youth

*T*he salty, metallic taste of blood was in John's mouth.

His face was drowning in earth and grass. The world was spinning, growing black. *Oh, please, God, save me*, he prayed. Far off, a voice said, "Who knows this dog's name?"

"He's John Bunyan of Elstow," answered a profane voice that sounded like Harry's.

"I thought he said he was from the town of Bedford," snarled the cavalier.

"I guess he'd rather be a dog from Bedford than a dog from Elstow," answered Harry.

"Say, are you being insolent too?"

"No, sire."

"I don't believe you."

John opened his eyes to see the cavalier whipping Harry, who was yelping and covering his head. Finally Harry collapsed. John realized the cavalier was looking at him again.

"If I hear the people of Bedfordshire were told about his majesty's troops by a John Bunyan, I'll come back for you, you insolent dog," said the cavalier, and he lashed John one more time. John drew his knees up and covered his head with his arms. Amid sounds of whipping he heard

Rogers whimpering for mercy. The cavalier was whipping Rogers to the ground too, as a warning. After a breathless silence, hoofbeats crashed near John's head, then diminished.

John sat up. "Let's go, men."

They rose, red-faced, dusty, and bruised. John retrieved his small peaked hat, punctured by the saber. By the time the boys finally reached the crossroads where one small road went on to the town of Bedford and one small road went on to the village of Elstow, John was calm and resolute. He turned up the road to Bedford.

"Where are you going?" asked Rogers nervously.

"I'm going into Bedford to tell everyone about the king's soldiers."

"Are you crazy?" screamed Harry.

"No point in arguing," said Rogers with a shrug of the shoulders as he followed John.

"Right," grumbled Harry, and followed too.

In Bedford John led the two boys up the road to Saint Mary's church, turned left onto High Street, crossed the bridge over the River Ouse and marched straight to the village Green. There in the cool afternoon among barren elm trees gentlemen stood about in earnest discussions.

John stood up on a bench, lifted his arms, and yelled, "Hear ye! Hear ye! Regiments of the king's army are crossing the river flats between here and Olney."

"Shut up, you lying brat!" Suddenly John was yanked off the bench by a man in a smart brown suit. "I saw you pass my estate in Kempston twice today, you scoundrels. It's a good thing I decided to follow you here."

Another man, even more resplendent in a green silk suit and plumed hat, approached. "What is the matter, Mister

Yarway?"

"Nothing, Sir Luke. It's just some lying brat from the country."

"I'm not lying—" John's words were cut off by a sharp blow to his head.

"Stop!" said Sir Luke. "This boy appears to be badly beaten. Have you done this, Mister Yarway?"

"Certainly not, Sir Luke."

"Then there might be some merit to his story," countered Sir Luke, "and I wish to hear it."

John told everyone in the green of the king's troops marching south. As he bitterly described the cavalier in detail he wiggled his finger through the saber hole in his hat. He waited with a deadpan face for their reaction.

"He's that scamp John Bunyan from Elstow," said one of the villagers, shaking his head.

"Still, he is covered with welts," said another.

Mister Yarway of Kempston held up his hand. "Yes, I admit the rascal is bruised a good bit, but he was probably beaten for stealing apples from a farmer's cellar or salmon from a fisherman's trunk along the river. He's a main suspect in these parts for every kind of mischief. He's nothing but the foul-mouthed son of a tinker."

Sir Luke studied him. "It seems you have a certain reputation, John Bunyan." Sir Luke addressed the crowd, "Even a rogue and the son of a tinker can tell the truth once in a while. And those welts don't lie. And neither does his description of the cavalier who flogged him." Sir Luke looked at a man nearby who appeared to be a soldier. "Colonel Cokayne, was there mingled in the depths of this boy's profanity an accurate description of a cavalier from a shire we all know is loyal to King Charles?"

"Indeed there was, sire," answered Colonel Cokayne. "The boy has described a cavalier of the shire of Nottingham to the north. We had best be getting back to the garrison at Newport Pagnell, Sir Luke."

Sir Luke looked at John one last time. "You must have some tiny spark of decency left in you, John Bunyan. See if you can tinder it." And Sir Luke left with Colonel Cokayne for Newport Pagnell, the parliamentary garrison ten miles west of Bedford.

John left the Green too, unabashed. He was used to being yelled at, even struck. The son of a tinker had no protectors. As to his foul mouth, he had always talked that way and couldn't change if he wanted to—which he did not. But he was disturbed by the cavalier, then Mister Yarway, turning on him. It always upset John when he found out someone he thought was nice was not nice after all. And yet John wasn't nice himself, and didn't intend to be—ever.

As the boys walked south down the High Road toward Elstow they approached the leper hospital of Saint Leonard. John snarled about faces eaten away and fingers falling off, but deep inside he always shuddered when he passed it. The few short years he had gone to free school in Bedford he had had to walk past the hospital every morning and every afternoon. School and the lepers were linked in his memory. He tried to forget them both, and because he couldn't, he made fun of them.

Harry continued on the High Road to Elstow. John and Rogers took a bridle path lined by willow trees across the fields to "Bunyan End." The Bunyans had lived out there so long in their wedge of land between two creeks everything was called "Bunyan this" and "Bunyan that." John's father, Thomas, seemed very proud of it, bragging that the

16

Bunyans had been there for three hundred years. John saw what it really meant. The fortunes of the Bunyans had declined generation after generation for hundreds of years. From landowners and innkeepers and brewers they had descended into lowly tinkers. They now owned nine acres and a cottage with one hearth.

They had almost reached the bottom of the pit. "Bunyan pit," mused John disrespectfully.

"Good-bye, John," said Rogers as he continued on to a neighboring cottage.

John grunted and went inside his father's cottage.

"Where have you been, John?" asked his mother, who looked twenty years older than her real age of thirty-nine. She was kneading bread dough. It should have been baked hours ago. But she was so weak. Some days she could hardly rise from her bed to spin and sew and launder and cook and clean and weed. "Where have you been?" repeated his mother.

"Out," growled John.

"You're all scuffed up, dear boy."

"I fell under a horse."

His mother ignored his sarcasm. "Your sister Margaret had to feed the chickens and hogs for you." Her voice was weary.

"Good. She'll go to heaven."

John thought his mother and sister Margie were soft. No matter how badly he treated them they still insisted on liking him—or anyone else for that matter. Now his father was not weak like that, just stupid. His father had had his whole life to better himself and he had not. He'd accumulated beatup brass and pewter utensils and bragged on them as if they were treasure. Everyone knew real treasure was gold or silver. And he had done nothing for John except send him to school for a few years, which was worthless. His father, who could barely scrawl the letters T. B., acted as if reading and writing were treasure too. John knew they were of no value at all if one had no money. Now Willie, his eight-year-old brother, was going to the free school.

At supper the five Bunyans sat on benches on both sides of a long table. Each one was hunched over a pewter plate, one hand clutching a knife and the other hand grasping for something to slice. The table held a large cartwheel of bread and a chunk of bacon with faint streaks of meat in the fat. In season his mother added soup of carrots or cabbage or turnips from her garden. Because they had no cow, only once in a while did they have milk or curds. Only rarely did they have roast beef. His mother once sang a ditty about how every poor wretch in England was supposed to enjoy beef for supper every Thursday and Sunday. "That must have been a time long ago," scoffed John.

John watched his father survey his wasteland of a table as if it flaunted a half carcass of beef and silver platters of fat pheasants.

All evening John grew angrier and angrier with his father. His father loved King Charles. So had John. Two months ago when Giles Thorne had been arrested in Bedford for praying publicly for King Charles at Saint Cuthbert Church John had raged against the Parliamentarians. But now Sir Samuel Luke, who supported Parliament, had been nice to John. John had heard of Sir Luke before. He was the one who had chased Sir Lewis Dyve out of Bedford. Sir Dyve supported King Charles, so

John had hated Sir Luke. But now Sir Luke seemed like a hero. And it seemed the king's men were not nice at all. So John was very angry with his father for leading him astray.

That night up in the loft of the cottage he writhed in terror. He was in hell and his skin was on fire. He was in torment. Somehow in his fevered mind he realized the flames had something to do with the welts on his skin, yet he had dreamed of hell many times before. All night he pleaded with sniggering devils for mercy, and all night they lashed him and kicked him. The cackling fiends were enmeshed in chains but still they were able to strike him again and again. He was so thirsty. . . .

John awoke to the rooster's crow, very angry with God. He remembered now. Hadn't he prayed for God's help when he'd been under the cavalier's whip? And hadn't God ignored him? And now once again he dreamed of hellfire. Well, if he had to go to hell, he wanted to be the tormentor, not the tormented. It seemed only natural if a boy was mean enough he might be very useful to the devil. And was there a meaner boy in Elstow than John?

"John?" called his father from below.

"Yes, I know," squawked John hatefully. "I'll do my chores." Of course he didn't intend to.

"Come down here," commanded his father. "You're going to do something different today."

The next days were a drastic change for John. His father made him an apprentice tinker. Whether his father did that because he heard about the ruckus in Bedford John did not know, nor did he care. Whether it was legal at his tender age he didn't know, nor did he care. To whom would he complain? All he knew was that now while his father ambled about the countryside mending any pot or kettle or

19

metal tool, John was supposed to be slaving in the back-yard of the cottage, hammering out the large jobs on the forge. And while a job was heating or cooling, John had to feed the hogs or chickens, or pull weeds in their tiny plot of wheat, or even grind flour from their puny store of wheat. He would have little time to wander now. But maybe his father wasn't that serious.

One evening his father came home and walked into the backyard. John had just returned from wandering the coun-tryside with his loyal gang. They had fought wicked King Charles all day. Softhearted Margie had fed the hogs and chickens for John. Willie had pulled weeds out of the wheat for him.

His father walked to the forge. "The forge is cold," he said.

"It cools fast, doesn't it?" answered John, adding a string of profanities.

"You're an apprentice now," said his father firmly and struck him. A second blow sent John tumbling to the ground. As John shook his head to regain his senses pain overwhelmed him. All his life his father had beaten him with a switch. Now he had flown into him with his fists.

"Those feathery taps won't keep me from roaming the shire with my men," he muttered after his father went inside the cottage. John had to get together with his gang. They were the only ones who understood how cruel his father was. They always took John's side, no matter what. Surely the devil would give John strength to persist. But the devil expected results. So John was soon scheming a return to Kempston Farm not only to create mischief for his new enemy Mister Yarway but to treat himself to what the gentry enjoyed.

A few days later John led his gang up the road to Bedford, then turned left to tromp west along the River Ouse. "Wicked Mister Yarway will never expect us to come this way," gloated John. "He'll be watching the road—if the numskull is watching anything but the end of his nose."

"What's that object among the reeds up there?" grunted Rogers, who always seemed to be looking off into the distance.

"A trunk holding some farmer's salmon?" ventured John. "Good. It's too dangerous to steal them because we might get caught carrying them, but we'll free them."

"Yes, it's definitely the right thing to do," added Harry maliciously.

John couldn't believe his luck as he approached the object in the reeds. It was not one of the great wicker trunks used to keep salmon. To a stake in the riverbank was tied a skiff. It didn't take an intelligent lad like John long to refine his devilish plan for mischief into a masterpiece. With the greatest caution they crept through a hedge to one of the cellars of Mister Yarway's farm. John had no intention of stealing apples. This time he was going to steal cheese. Real cheddar cheese. The thought of it made his mouth water.

"Say, this skiff is very wobbly," complained Rogers after they returned from the cellar to load stolen blocks of cheese into the craft.

"So what?" snarled John.

"I can't swim."

"Neither can I," replied John. "but that isn't going to keep me from floating the skiff down the river to a spot near Fenlake."

21

"Do you mean you're going to take this skiff right past the eyes of every soul in Bedford?" asked Rogers, stunned.

"Certainly. We'll cover the cheese with weeds. The town folks are too dense to know what is happening. We'll unload our booty near Fenlake, which is no more than a mile from my house. Of course I'll not take the cheese inside my house. I'll dig a hole and hide my share near the forge." And he added bitterly, "Now that my dear father no longer uses it."

"Don't you think you ought to test the skiff first?" suggested Harry contemptuously. "What if you can't pilot it?"

John led by example. Arguing with lesser lights tried his patience too much. He jumped into the skiff, got his balance in the wobbly craft, then picked up a long pole. He stabbed the pole into the grassy bank and shoved. The skiff glided out into the river.

"Still scared witless, Rogers?" goaded John. "Still confounded by the difficulties, Harry?"

"Now bring it back," said Harry in a disrespectful voice.

John jabbed the pole into the water. The murky river was deeper than he'd expected, and he had to bend awkwardly over the side. Then as he shoved on the pole he discovered it was stuck fast in the mud bottom. In a moment he knew he had made a great mistake, maybe his last. He fell into the river.

Oh, God, I can't swim! he screamed silently.

three

A Proud Musketeer

John thrashed the water madly. *Oh, no. If there is a God in heaven, save me.* Water choked him already. He kicked his feet, flailed his arms. The icy river sucked life from his body. Water was inside his head, stinging him under the eyes. His chest was collapsing in agony. His arm struck something. It was the side of the boat. It had floated back to him. He clung to it, coughing water from his mouth and nose. Suddenly his bare feet hit the muddy bottom. He lunged to the shore, letting the skiff drift away. He crawled onto the bank, flopped on his stomach and coughed water for a long time. His body trembled from the chill and the closeness of the grave.

"Let's get out of here," he finally rasped with a very sore throat. "We can't use the skiff now."

"Yes, let's go," agreed Rogers.

"I guess I've had enough cheese for one day," commented a bored Harry, who appeared to have been stuffing cheese in his mouth all the while John shivered and heaved water from his lungs.

John got home in time to fire up the forge and hammer a new edge on a plowshare. Margie had fed the hogs and chickens for him. Somehow the exertion over the forge felt good. His father shook his head at the small amount of work John had done but didn't beat him. That night John

23

slept very little. He had come seconds from going to hell. And yet he was alive. Had the devil saved him? Or had God? And if God had saved him, why had He? John knew why the devil would save him. John had become his servant in this world.

The next day John stuck by the forge. And the day after that he was there too. Labor felt oddly satisfying. And he needed time to think. The year before, his grandfather Bunyan had died. The old man, who had fancied himself a merchant so much he called himself a "petty chapman," but had never been more than an itinerant peddler, was survived by his fourth wife; John's real grandmother Bunyan had died the same year his father was born. No one talked about it, but John thought maybe his grandmother had died giving birth to his father. That was certainly common enough around Elstow. And somehow it fit his father's cruel nature. John's other grandparents were dead too. Grandmother Bentley's pruney face and watery eyes he could remember vaguely, but Grandfather Bentley was buried in the past, as deep and faceless as his real grandmother Bunyan. But what difference did it make whether they had died recently or long ago? That entire generation was dead, and they would soon be forgotten like every other family member in the old times. There was nothing to distinguish them. Nothing.

"And where are those forgotten souls now?" John wondered aloud. "Heaven or hell?"

John had been forced to go to Elstow Church since he could remember. That was about the only thing he couldn't blame on his father. Attending parish church every week was the law of England. Pastor Christopher Hall made it plain enough that the dead were either in heaven or in hell.

Neither place excited John much in broad daylight. He was sure he had lost his chance to go to heaven long ago. He tried to tell himself hell was about as desirable as heaven because he was surely going to go there.

"But if I'm going to earn the right to serve the devil as a tormentor I must get back to my evil deeds," he reminded himself.

A few days later he met with his gang, anxious to plot new mischief and tell them how persecuted he was at home, but all they would talk about was the war. On October 23, 1642, two great armies had met—just twenty miles southwest of Elstow—at Edgehill. That was where the men they saw marching must have eventually fought. Thirty thousand men clashed, mutilating each other with swords and pikes and axes and musket balls. Sir Luke was there too and survived, but five thousand men had spent their last blood in the soil. When it was all over, King Charles withdrew his army west to the heavy fortress of Oxford. Lord Essex withdrew his army of the Parliament south to their stronghold: London. Both sides claimed victory.

"The country is split in half," fretted Rogers.

Harry added, "The king controls the northwest and Parliament controls the southeast."

"Our shire of Bedford is on the frontier between the warring halves," worried Rogers.

"It's too bad soldiers have to be sixteen," lamented John. "The war will be over before we reach sixteen." He added dreamily, "What a chance for pure devilry. . . ."

After the battle at Edgehill, rumors came back about other battles. First, the army of the Parliament lost to the king's army at Adwalton Moor. Then the army of the

Parliament met the king's army at Roundway Downs in a showdown between Parliament's best general, William Waller, and the king's champion, Prince Rupert. Waller was thrashed by Prince Rupert. Bedford and the shires to the east had cast their lot with the rebel Parliament. John worried less and less about the war ending too soon.

"Maybe the devil will bring the war to me," he told himself.

One month before John's fifteenth birthday he worked on his father's forge in the backyard, indulging in black thoughts. It had rained heavily and the creek nearest the cottage had overflowed as it always did. The field behind the cottage was a muddy slough. According to English law anyone's livestock could graze any field lying fallow. So it seemed all the hogs in Elstow were wallowing in the Bunyan slough up to their snouts. John had to smell their stench and hear their grunts and squeals all day.

When Rogers ran breathlessly into the backyard he was like a burst of sunshine. "The king's cavalry under Sir Lewis Dyve are raiding Bedford!" he gasped.

"Sir Luke will thrash Sir Dyve," answered John calmly.

"No. I heard the king's men are winning."

John let the mule shoe drop out of the tongs into the fire. "Let's go to Bedford, Rogers."

"Wh—wh—what if that cavalier from Nottingham is there? He said he would come back to get you!"

John snorted. Whether he was going to fight or watch he never said. His mother begged him not to go. Margie begged him not to go. Rogers begged him not to go. But the thing that stopped him was his father's fist. By the time John slipped away to Bedford later, with Harry, the king's men were gone and the citizens of Bedford wandered the streets in a daze. Sir Dyve, who had escaped Sir Luke the previous year only by swimming the River Ouse, had returned with a vengeance—and hundreds of cavaliers. They routed the smaller force of cavalry from Newport Pagnell and plundered the town of 2,000. Bodies covered with sheets lined High Street all the way from St. Peter's Green to St. John's Hospital.

"That's the way with this war now," said one of the citizens. "When one party goes out to siege, and the other side gets wind of it, then they come to their homebase to plunder and kill. Sir Dyve must have known Sir Luke was away from Newport Pagnell on his own raiding party."

Each shire had some recalcitrants fighting for the other side and holding out in their fortified estates. Even Elstow had such a holdout. In January of 1644, a party of 100 left the parliamentary garrison at Newport Pagnell and marched into Elstow. There they arrested the Royalist living in Hillersdon House near Elstow Church and dragged him away. The day was so bitterly cold and it happened so fast that few people witnessed it, certainly not John, who lived over a mile distant.

That winter was the coldest in John's memory. Rumors came to Elstow that Londoners were allowed to cut any tree within thirty miles of the great city. It was no coincidence they first hacked down every tree in the king's splendid forest at Windsor Castle. At the cottage John was supposed to go down to the river every day and forage for wood along the bank. But many days he simply played at the river with his gang. He knew his mother and Margie would brave the cold and scrounge wood if he did not bring enough back. And they would not tell his father about it. John was happier to see spring than any time in

27

his life. His mother, and even Margie, coughed a lot and seemed worn out.

"You two need rest," said John.

"Will you help us around the cottage, John?" asked his mother hopefully.

"Don't I always?" he answered defensively.

In the first week of May the annual four-day fair in Elstow drew people from all over the shires. Except for trading at fairs, merchants were not allowed to trade in towns other than their own—it was the law of England. But John wasn't attracted by trade. He wasn't drawn by the jugglers, puppeteers, play actors, or bonfires either. He delighted in the dim-lit fields beyond the main fairway. His heart sang to the flutes and fiddles. Evil reigned there in cockfights, wild dancing, card games, and painted women whose purpose he could only imagine, because he had no money. But just watching what he would someday enjoy lifted his spirits.

"How the devil knows how to enjoy life!" he told Harry.

John's mother became very ill in June. At first he paid little attention. Most country women were sick a lot. It was a very hard life. But soon she remained in bed. "My poor weak mother," he mumbled to himself. Now Margie had to bake the bread and do a dozen other chores. John was far more interested in the fact that King Charles himself had been less than twenty miles south of Elstow, raiding the town of Leighton. Grudgingly, John began to like the king again.

"The stuttering sot is keeping the war going," rejoiced John to his gang one evening.

"My stepfather says King Charles is a sleepy-eyed fop," added Harry maliciously.

"But the fop fights," said John devilishly. "We might get into a battle or two yet. Why is your face as white as cow's milk, Rogers?"

When John's mother developed a fever, he began to worry. Many people died from fever. What would their home be like without his mother? She no longer seemed weak, but precious to him. He felt so bad he prayed for her. But one day she was alive sipping broth and the next day she was as still and cold and ashen as stone. His sweet mother was dead. Once again, God had let him down. At the side of the grave he hardly noticed his mother's brother John or her sisters Rose, Elizabeth, Annie, and Mary. His father's well-dressed brother Edward was there too. And so were his father's three sisters. John's sister Margie, who was sickly now herself, tried to comfort him. But John brushed her off. He had a knot deep inside that hurt. It had something to do with the way he had treated his mother.

When Margie died the following month John felt as if his world was ending. He had prayed for Margie too, but of course God had failed him again. What he got instead of deliverance for sweet, red-haired, freckled Margie were more dreams of hell for himself and more pain deep inside. It had something to do with the way he had treated Margie.

A few days later John and his gang heard in Bedford that the greatest battle of the war had been fought far to the north, at Marston Moor, near York. There the army of the Parliament routed the king's army. The battle was turned from defeat to victory by a cavalry general named Oliver Cromwell, so invincible the soldiers dubbed him Ironsides.

Harry was wide-eyed. "They say Ironsides grew up just a hike down the River Ouse from us—at Huntingdon."

"I can't believe I once embarrassed myself by being a Royalist," muttered John to himself. "That's one more thing I can thank my father for. Besides working my mother and sister to death." And as John reaped wheat and stacked it in sheaves in their tiny field he sulked because the war would soon be over. Surely the devil was behind this greatest calamity in the history of England, and John would miss it.

His life became even bleaker. While John brought in the sheaves of wheat to thresh them and sack the grain, his father brought a new bride into the cottage. As John lay up in the loft at night with aching muscles, mourning his mother and sister, his father slept with his new bride, Anne, below. How John hated his father. How he longed for the devil to keep the war going.

A few weeks later in November—after John had plowed the tiny field and sown new wheat, all without a mule because his father needed the mule to return home from his tinkering all the faster to his new bride—John's day of deliverance came. With no more than a grunt of farewell to his stepmother Anne, John left the cottage. Rogers spotted him walking down the bridle path toward Bedford, with Willie, and yelled, "Where are you going, John?"

"I'm taking young master William to school."

"But you never do that, John," said Rogers, gawking. "And why are you carrying the knapsack?"

"If you must know, I'm joining the army. I'm sixteen today, Rogers."

"So am I. Why don't you wait until the authorities call for you?"

"The war might be over by then." He marched on, knowing Rogers could not understand why he wanted to be in a war. He merely grunted as teary-eyed Willie tried to say good-bye at the school. He had always regarded Willie as too young to understand anything. Later, when John entered the gates of the garrison at Newport Pagnell he felt as if he had been freed. Now he would serve in the army right along side Oliver Cromwell, old "Ironsides" himself.

The garrison held nearly a thousand men from all the shires to the east. Idle talk soon told him the men at Newport Pagnell had seen a lot of combat. They had fought all around in shires held by Royalists. The commander was none other than Sir Samuel Luke himself. He betrayed no memory of John. In fact, in the days that followed, John rarely saw him. The officers he saw occasionally were Colonel Cokayne and Major Ennis.

After all the new men had been drilled in marching for a few days, John's sergeant came to him and said, "Bunyan, it's time we decided where you fit best in this army of the Parliament."

"I prefer to ride in Ironside's cavalry, sir."

The sergeant laughed. "The cavalry is not for the likes of you. You're a good-sized fellow though. Are you as strong as you look?"

"My father used me for a mule."

"I was going to make you a pikeman but because you have some wit I will make you a musketeer."

John was delighted to be a musketeer. The pikeman not only lugged an unwieldy sixteen-foot razor-sharp pike, but wore a helmet, tassets over the thighs, and plates over the chest and back—all of heavy steel. Yet as John put on his gear he realized the musketeer was heavily encumbered too, not only with weight but with awkwardness. The matchlock musket, which weighed twenty pounds, and the

31

long sword in a scabbard were only the beginning. He also carried a long forked iron rod called a rest, in which he would steady the musket. Adding to his burden, a powder-horn and pouch of lead musket balls hung across his chest. Also dangling from a bandoleer across his chest were pouches with wads and primer.

But his uniform thrilled him. His shiny black shoes were brand-new. He wore a wide, floppy tan hat with a white plume. Over white hose were tan knee-length trousers. His white, long-sleeved shirt had a wide collar turned down over his scarlet vest. The tan bandoleer piped in scarlet accented everything perfectly. John had never dressed so well in his life. Every article was finer than anything he had ever worn. It did seem odd the shires could raise money for such fine things when war was involved, yet could not spare a half-penny for the poor. But so much the better, he reflected. The devil was at work everywhere.

One day Major Ennis addressed the new men, "We are the New Model Army, the most advanced army in the world. Thanks to Oliver Cromwell your pay is standard and all regulations are spelled out. Listen to me well: the pikeman is the musketeer's best friend, and the musketeer is the pikeman's best friend. If you don't believe me now, you will believe me after you fight your first battle."

John practiced marching in the heavy gear day after day. Occasionally he got to fire his musket, but powder and balls were precious. The sergeant taught him how to prop the musket straight up between his knees, measure just the right amount of powder into his palm, then dump it into the end of the barrel. Then he dropped a lead ball down the barrel and inserted a paper wad. With a ramrod he shoved the wad tightly against the ball and powder. Then he steadied the musket in the rest, lit his rope match, sprinkled primer in the flashpan, aimed down the barrel, and pulled the matchlock. A moment after the flashpan burst into flame there was a deafening explosion and smoke billowed from the barrel. The lead ball was supposed to smash into a wooden target. Occasionally it did. But John never saw anything through all the smoke.

"Now I know why you are my best friend," John said to a pikeman. "I can fire only one shot every couple of minutes. The rest of the time I'm completely vulnerable while I'm loading for another shot." And John warmed to the thought of being protected within a thicket of bristling sixteen-foot pikes.

John also learned the importance of Newport Pagnell. The garrison was a good portion of the "Eastern Association," one of Parliament's three armies. Oliver Cromwell's own son had been there and remained there yet—moldering deep in the black earth. He had died of smallpox only the previous year. As if to prove the garrison was snaring every young man around, Harry and Rogers soon arrived. But they were put in other companies more green than John's and he hardly knew they were there.

A new soldier learned many things about English life in the garrison. One of his first days there John asked some soldiers, "Where do they train the cavalry?"

"Fool, except for our officers you won't see any of the gentry or nobility among us," answered one soldier. "They are too good for the likes of us. And after we skewer King Charles, we'll skewer them too, no matter whose side they fight for now."

John, who had always reveled in his rebellious attitude,

33

was outdone at Newport Pagnell. He had never heard such disrespect and foul language. And somehow hostility in others always shocked him. These soldiers maligned everything: the food, the king, the nobles, the gentry, the local girls, the officers, the pay—even God.

"The Bible ain't true at all," said one soldier.

"Not true?" John felt as if he had been slapped in the face, even though he had never willingly read one word of the "Soldiers' Pocket Bible" that had been issued to him as well as every other soldier.

"There ain't no God," said the soldier named Brown.

"No God?" gasped John.

And that night in his bunk he worried. *No God. Didn't that mean no devil either? Nothing?* That hideous possibility slithered through his mind for the first time. He felt like a fool. In all his rebellion he had never thought such a horrifying possibility. Hell almost seemed like salvation compared to nothing. Nothing. Oblivion. To the end of time. He could not comprehend that. He swallowed hard and tried to sleep.

No God. No devil. Nothing. . . .

four

A Solemn Soldier

*J*ohn's education continued day after day at the garrison as he listened to opinions he had either never heard before or had heard but not understood. For the first time in his life he realized that the Church of England retained many Roman Catholic elements in its hierarchy and service. Religious people trying mightily to purify the Church of England of those elements came to be called Puritans. On the other hand another group vying against the hierarchy of bishops of the Church of England was called Presbyterian, for people who wanted to run the church with local presbyters or elders.

"In the garrison we have many Puritans and Presbyterians," said the soldier named Brown. "And even though they both profess to love their brothers, neither group trusts the other," he added cynically.

And there were small radical groups. Levelers were people who wanted to do away with the nobility and gentry. Diggers went beyond levelers, insisting on dividing up all wealth in order to create heaven on earth for everyone. Ranters encompassed several dissident groups. Some challenged the truth of the Bible, even the existence of God. Some Ranters believed in Christ, yet said He was a mystical force inside a person, and He never was an historical figure at all. Still more Ranters took the stance of Calvin to the extreme: because God had predestined those who were to be saved it made no difference whatever how a person behaved. They were either of God's "elect" or they were not. Because of this view some Ranters were often shockingly immoral—even in John's eyes.

The soldier named Brown sounded like a Ranter to John. One day John asked him, "If you don't believe in the king or the Parliament or God, who do you fight for?"

"My neck. I didn't volunteer for this. I was conscripted. And don't ask me why I stay. Don't you know our friend Cromwell is hanging deserters now?"

Yet Brown did desert a few days later. The garrison had learned a party was going forth from Newport Pagnell to siege the fortified estate of a Royalist in the shire of Gloucester. John was scheduled to go, but a friendly boy named Hazelwood who was from that area begged John to let him go in his place. When the party returned a few weeks later John learned Hazelwood had been killed while standing sentry. A musket ball had gone right through his brain.

"That should have been me," John muttered to himself. "Is living or dying in battle nothing but pure luck?"

He was no longer so eager to fight. He knew by now that conscientious soldiers were killed right next to careless soldiers. Strong were killed next to weak. Brilliant were killed next to stupid. Musket balls zipped through the air all over the battlefield as random and mindless as shooting stars. The more he thought about it the surer he became that living or dying in battle was pure luck. And if there was no heaven or hell why would a sane man risk his one and only life? He found himself hoping the war would soon end. Maybe he would be spared.

As if John's newly educated fear was not cancerous enough, his courage was ravaged by talk of the prowess of their enemy, especially the invincible leader of the king's cavalry, Prince Rupert. "He's the work of the devil," claimed one soldier. "He sneaks right inside our garrisons and counts heads."

"He has unnatural powers," shuddered another soldier. "The king lets Prince Rupert's cavalry have the first thrust in every battle. And Prince Rupert always draws blood."

"Why not? He can make himself invisible," insisted the first soldier. "He can speak in tongues. He can prophesy. Even his white dog, Boy, is a demon."

As the weeks passed, John Bunyan wanted less and less of war. Then one dawn in late May of 1645 came words from John's sergeant that chilled his heart. "Get all your gear together, men. We're marching."

As John prepared his gear he was presented with a metal helmet like the ones pikemen wore. "What's this for?"

"A new regulation. From now on, all musketeers wear metal helmets in battle."

They struck out due west, wading mile after mile through fields of knee-high green wheat and clomping across wooden bridges. Their officer was Major Ennis. It was many hours before the men heard the rumor they were going to Leicester, a city forty miles northwest of Newport Pagnell.

"This ain't the way to Leicester," snarled one soldier.

"It is if you have to avoid the whole blooming king's army," snapped another.

"This won't be a small skirmish," sighed John's pike-man, a youth only one year older, but a veteran who had

37

been in battle before. He was Gibbs, the son of a cooper in Bedford. "God help us, friend Bunyan."

Dread crept over John. Where were Oliver Cromwell and the rest of Parliament's armies? Even Sir Samuel Luke was not going with them. As a matter of fact, they had no cavalry going with them either. Nor any cannon. Not even Colonel Cokayne. Why should he? He commanded a regiment. Marching with John were probably no more than two troops, maybe 120 men. Were they being thrown away?

By afternoon they reached the dense forest of Whittlewood. Then they struck north, keeping just inside the edge of the forest. They had marched almost twenty miles that day. Ten miles, with all the gear they carried, was considered a hard day's march. They camped that night among the trees. No fires were allowed.

Gibbs sighed, "Now I won't be able to read my Holy Scripture."

John knew Gibbs owned a complete Bible. It was rare to see a common man read the pocket version, still rarer to find one who read a complete Bible. And John wondered, Why would Gibbs want to read a Bible anyway? John had certainly never read his, and wondered if he could still read at all.

They marched among the trees all the next day and camped again in woods, now called Leighfield Forest. Again they were allowed no fires. It was pitch black when their sergeant roused them to continue marching, but John knew they had left the forest for open fields when he felt wheat brushing his legs. It was not yet dawn when they stood before an entrance on one of the great walls surrounding Leicester.

"Let them know we're friendly or God help us," muttered Gibbs.

A series of gates had to be raised to allow entry. John shuddered as the great barriers creaked and groaned upward. He felt sick as he clomped over wooden logs inside the gateway that he knew were trapdoors over deep cruel pits. The hair stood up on his neck as he remembered all the "murder holes" in the stone archway over their heads that could unleash boiling oil and a dozen other ways of killing a man, all excruciatingly painful.

They hurried over cobbled streets past a few frightened citizens holding lamps. At what someone said was the new south wall of Leicester they climbed stairs to a platform that allowed them to look out embrasures in the wall to the countryside to the south. John removed his helmet and felt as if his head would float away. A breeze caressed his face. He didn't have to march his aching feet any more. He had the wall on which to lean and rest his musket. He squinted into blackness.

"Rest while you can, friend Bunyan," said his pikeman, Gibbs, clanking his metal against the wall as he sat down. "You can't see anything now anyway."

John sat down with his back to the wall too. Yes, that was better. Maybe the whole thing was just a mistake. Perhaps the king's army was not out there at all. When dawn light came he would look out on a vast green plain. There would be nothing in sight but a few red deer. And as the black sky ever so slowly brightened he convinced himself more and more the king's army was nowhere near Leicester. Gibbs was snoring. *He is a veteran*, thought John, *sleeping because he knows the whole thing was a silly mistake*. John felt like laughing.

As dawn light flooded the field south of the wall John was back on his feet. He had an excellent view of vast green fields bordered by the long shadows of forest. "Nothing," he said, soothing himself.

"What are you muttering about?" asked Gibbs, trying to shake off sleep. "What do you see?"

"Nothing. But you already knew that. Otherwise, how could you sleep?"

"I slept because I'm safe in God's hands no matter what happens."

"We were lucky to get their new wall," enthused John. Their platform had an identical protective wall with embrasures facing the inside of the city. "Look. We can defend ourselves up here even if the enemy gets inside the city. Not that it matters much now, since the enemy is nowhere in sight."

Gibbs sighed. "Friend Bunyan, I hope you are right."

"Gibbs, what is that odd-looking fence over there in the distance at the edge of the forest?" asked John. "It must be half a mile wide."

"Fence?" The pikeman rose, rubbing his aching muscles. He groaned, "The king's men cleared the timber and used it to build a barricade for their artillery."

"Do you mean cannons are hidden behind that barricade?"

"Certainly," replied Gibbs.

"Cannons!" gasped John without knowing it. He grabbed his heavy helmet and put it on.

John watched the fence, while Gibbs rested and read his Bible. There was nothing to do but wait. For a while John would convince himself there would be no attack; the enemy often broke off a siege for reasons the besieged never knew. Then, for a while John would despair. In a few hours he could be dead. He could be plunged into oblivion. Forever. Life and death were pure chance.

"How can you sit there and read?" he asked Gibbs angrily.

"This book is the greatest good news a man can have, friend Bunyan."

John grumbled and watched the distant fence every moment. Even after a soldier came to pass out bread and cheese for lunch John watched the fence as the food went down his throat like sand. His head was hot under the helmet but he would not take it off. It was the middle of the afternoon when movement caught his eye.

"Look!" gasped John. "Cavalry have come out of the forest. They are racing up and down in front of the fence." As he watched, more and more horsemen joined the spectacle. "There must be five hundred men on horses!"

"Warming up their steeds," said Gibbs, now standing, in a voice so resigned John had to look at him. Gibbs looked as if someone had kicked him in the stomach. "They don't care if we know their plan now or not," continued Gibbs. "They think we can't stop them. After the cannonballs bombard our wall into rubble, their cavalry will charge through the breach, led by Prince Rupert."

"Prince Rupert?" John's mouth was as dry as chalk dust. "Rubble? This very wall where we stand?"

John watched with Gibbs as more cavaliers raced their horses. There were now thousands of them. A moment before John heard the first boom of a cannon he heard the iron ball whomp into soft earth somewhere south of his wall. "It's fallen far short," he crowed happily.

"They'll be watching with a telescope," commented

41

Gibbs. "The next ball will be closer."

John saw the next ball hit the packed earth closer to the wall, then roll to a stop against the wall. It was followed two minutes later by a cracking splintering sound. That ball had struck the lower part of the wall. Dislodged stone lay at the foot of the wall. In the distance smoke began to waft up from behind the barricade.

"Better get behind the merlon," said his pikeman. "Rest. It will be some time before they get all the cannons adjusted."

John sat with his back against the wall. Again, there was nothing to do but wait. Prince Rupert's cavalry had moved aside to wait too. Balls thudded against the wall with regularity now. At first John leaned forward so the horrid destruction wouldn't vibrate from the wall through his bones. But after a while he leaned back and accepted the shuddering inevitability. John now knew from the sound where they struck. There were no longer any soft earth thuds, only deep whonks for strikes on the lower part of the wall and high-pitched cracks higher on the wall.

"They are going to breach the wall not a hundred yards from where we are, friend Bunyan," said Gibbs.

Shouts of dismay at the crumbling wall were occasionally pierced by screams of agony. Men were being sliced and bruised by stone fragments. And men were yelling that the wall was being breached! The bombardment seemed to go on forever. When would Prince Rupert charge? John suddenly realized he would soon be aiming his musket at a real living man. He would be trying to take the very breath of life away from that man. And that man would be trying to kill him. John felt very sick.

"Gibbs! Get down here," screamed their sergeant. "We

need to rebuild the wall."

"Praise the good Lord above I won't use my weapon," said Gibbs. He patted John on the hand and moved toward the stairs. The sergeant told several other pikemen to go below. John felt very alone now. Gibbs was like an anchor in a violent storm for him.

Suddenly the sergeant stared hard at John. "You too, Bunyan! Leave your gear. We need your strong back now a lot more than your musket!"

John unbuckled his scabbard with the long sword and let it drop to the parapet. Then he disentangled himself from his powderhorn and pouches of lead musket balls, wads, and primer. He stumbled down the stairs, numb. All his training to shoot a musket was thrown aside. He would be a beast of burden. But what difference did it make in such madness? He caught up with Gibbs. They approached a mountain of rubble. They scrambled into the rubble to fumble and stumble as they tried to rebuild the wall, explosions and zinging of stone fragments in their ears.

John's hands were raw and bleeding as he lugged the pieces of stone higher. Men abruptly fell from the pile of rubble like rag dolls. John himself had to carry a man away from the rubble. The man's face was white as flour. Blood bubbled from his chest. Away from the wall a woman bent over to tend the man as John stood and gawked.

"Back to the breach, you lazy dog!" screamed an officer at John and shoved him sprawling.

Screams and musket fire up on the wall told him the cavalry had charged. But John kept working. This was to be his role for this battle—until he was killed. He carried stones and bleeding bodies. Blood was all over his uniform. Blood was everywhere, mixed in stone powder. A great cheer went up on the wall.

"The cavalry has broken off its attack!" yelled someone on the parapet.

Soon John realized it was dark. Again, the cavalry charged. Again, a great cheer told John the enemies were repulsed. Sometime later the cavalry charged again. John found he no longer cared. It was obvious now he would not survive. And that fact brought him no dread at all. He was numb to all feeling. In the darkness he was as likely to grab a dead man's head as a stone. Dead bodies were lying everywhere.

"Get up the stairs!" screamed someone.

Up on the parapet once again, he finally found his gear in the blackness. "What's going on?" he screamed at a man who he thought was Gibbs because he clanked around in the armor of a pikeman.

"The king's men are inside the city!" It was Gibbs.

"Aren't we going to surrender?"

"The longer we hold out the better terms we can negotiate for ourselves—up to a point."

John knew only too well what Gibbs meant. Sometimes soldiers held out too long. If they caused a lot of deaths the enemy considered unnecessary, then nothing could save them. They would all be "put to the sword" after they were defeated.

"What time is it?" grumbled John.

Gibbs looked up at the stars. "Some time after midnight."

"We've been fighting for nine or so hours." It seemed a lifetime. And it had been for many an unlucky soldier.

Somewhere farther down the wall by a lantern men were yelling back and forth. There was no anger in the voices, only earnest reason.

"Major Ennis is negotiating," murmured Gibbs. "Thank God for such a good man."

After a while John heard his sergeant's voice, "Get your gear together, men. We're going over the breach. And keep your mouths shut. The king's troops are coming into the city by the north gate!"

The next hours were rough. Men like John who were only slightly wounded had to carry the more severely wounded. It was many hours later and almost dawn as they struggled into the forests southeast of Leicester. John finally felt free to talk to Gibbs. "How did we escape so easily?"

"We didn't escape. Major Ennis negotiated our release. If we hadn't fought so long and so hard Prince Rupert wouldn't have agreed, but he didn't want to fight us another day or two from the south wall. And he knew Major Ennis would do it."

They slept several hours in the forest, then spent an entire day dressing wounds and resting. Litters were made for the severely wounded. After another night's sleep they buried those who had died in the night and then moved on. Instead of staying in the forest for cover, as they had done before, they struck out straight across rolling fields of wheat for Northampton. On the second day of June they marched back into Newport Pagnell. In the next days John laundered, then sewed his tattered uniform.

By then, the garrison was buzzing with rumors. The king's men had raped and plundered Leicester—after they had executed some of its defenders! Now King Charles was sauntering south to Oxford, commandeering livestock and grain, even stopping near Daventry to hunt deer. Then John heard Oliver Cromwell was in Bedford with 700 of

45

his horsemen!

"Someone must warn him King Charles is just northwest of here with 9,000 men," said John.

"Tell Ironsides yourself," laughed Gibbs and pointed east to rising dust. "There he comes."

Oliver Cromwell and his cavalry camped by the River Ouse. Sir Samuel Luke went out to confer with Cromwell. The men in the garrison could only squint into the distant camp and wonder if one of the men they saw was Ironsides himself. The next day Cromwell and his men rode northwest.

"He's going right at the king," gasped John.

John's sergeant approached. "All able-bodied soldiers are marching," he said.

John and Gibbs found themselves marching northwest, still all bruises and scabs, but rested. By June 13, they marched into Kislingbury, just eight miles from Daventry. The sight took John's breath away. Battle flags flew everywhere.

"It's a colossal army!" exclaimed John.

"And praise God it's ours, and not the king's," said Gibbs, with a sigh of relief.

Yes, it was not the army of King Charles. It was the parliamentary army of Lord Fairfax. Within hours the great army that men said numbered 14,000 to 15,000 lumbered north toward the village of Naseby.

John's sergeant was unusually talkative. "The king's army is moving northeast. They've heard about us. They're trying to get back to Leicester. But they're going to have to stop and fight us. Very soon, men."

Just across the Avon River, on Mill Hill, Lord Fairfax set up his parliamentary army in the false dawn. Infantry forces under Philip Skippon were in the center in two lines. John was in the second of those lines. On his right were Oliver Cromwell and 3,600 horsemen in two lines. On John's left was a similar wing of horsemen under Henry Ireton.

As the sun rose, John looked across a valley to the north at Dust Hill and saw the glittering army of King Charles! His army was a mirror image of John's own. Directly in front of John was infantry under Jacob Astley. Opposing Cromwell was the cavalry of Langdale. Opposing Ireton was the cavalry of Prince Rupert!

"Rupert charges!" screamed a soldier near John.

Of course it was Prince Rupert who charged on one side, and Cromwell who charged on the other. John had no time to enjoy the spectacle. The Royalist infantry was attacking in the center. The line of parliamentary infantry in front of him was falling apart. He was amazed at how few shots were fired. He fired only one shot himself, never seeing through the smoke if his ball hit anything, and was suddenly in a melee of swinging musket butts, ripping pikes and slashing swords.

John quickly threw his musket aside and slashed with his sword. How long he fought he had no idea. Whether he actually brought down another soldier he didn't know. It was shoulder to shoulder chaos. Suddenly he was knocked aside like a leaf in a whirlwind. Great warhorses plowed though the foot soldiers.

"It's our own Ironsides!" screamed the infantry.

Oliver Cromwell's horsemen slashed the Royalists mercilessly. Within minutes the Royalist infantrymen who still survived had surrendered. Only later in the day did John hear what had turned the tide of battle. Prince Rupert had smashed Ireton's wing, and chased them from the field and beyond. Cromwell had smashed Langdale's wing and driven them from the field too. But the disciplined Cromwell did not chase them. He turned his mighty force on the scuffling infantries. By the time Prince Rupert returned his cavalry to the field, the Royal army had surrendered!

"It seems Ironsides has an iron will too," observed John.

More and more reports of total victory poured in. Parliament had captured the entire baggage train of King Charles, all his powder, his cannons, and his entire infantry of 5,000 men! It was time to celebrate. The whole aspect of the war had changed. The king would never recover from such a disaster. Only he and his cavalry had escaped to Leicester.

"Why are you so downcast?" asked John of Gibbs.

"Haven't you heard how we slaughtered common foot soldiers trying to escape along the road to the north?"

"Surely they were fighting us as we pursued them."

"I hope so," said Gibbs glumly.

But the next morning John saw for himself. He and Gibbs were in a burial detail sent along the road north of the battlefield. The dead soldiers had no weapons. One officer in their burial detail explained the weapons had been picked up already. Yet some of the dead had money on them. Among the dead soldiers was a sight that iced John's heart as it had not been chilled since Margie's funeral. One corpse could not have been a soldier. How could it be?

"A woman!" he gasped to Gibbs nearby.

48

five

A Flower in the Field

"A woman?" puzzled Gibbs from a grave he was digging. "Are you sure?"

John knelt over a tangle of long flowing gray fabric. With trembling fingers he pulled aside a fold of gray. Revealed was a redheaded, freckle-faced doll. She appeared to have fainted. Yet her cheek was bloodless and as cold as the earth. When it came time to carry the poor woman to the grave, he saw the hidden side of her head was smashed like a melon.

"How can this be?" he asked Gibbs.

"She was an Irish woman who followed the soldiers," barked one of the officers.

The horror mounted. They found more women, more smashed skulls. Always the explanation was as senseless. Gibbs was not saying anything. There must be a reason to keep silent. So John remained silent too. But he saw a new look in his pikeman's eyes: rage.

The graves along the road to Leicester were marked only by fresh mounds of earth. They would be forever the unnamed dead. Many victims had been buried together. John, now a true veteran of carnage, stumbled along the road not wanting to tally up the total. But in his heart he knew there had been at least several hundred dead, and worst of all, probably at least one hundred were women.

Later, in Market Harborough, where the Royal infantry was being guarded, John saw among their wounded soldiers dozens of women with faces swathed in bloody rags. And the story unfolded: every woman with the king's troops was deemed a prostitute; if she was thought to be Irish she was brained with a battle ax; if she was thought to be English her face was disfigured with a knife.

"It's too consistent to be spontaneous," John grumbled to Gibbs later. "Some officer must have ordered it."

"How did all this happen, friend Bunyan?" answered Gibbs in a thin voice. "How did we come to fight on a side that murders women?"

They heard from some soldiers that such terrible vengeance was justified because of the execution of the defenders of Leicester—not to mention the rape of the poor women there and the plundering of every cottage.

Truth seemed to crystallize in Gibbs' face. "Our officers are of the gentry and nobility. These women are common folk like us."

Gibbs worried John now. "You have the look of a man about to desert," whispered John. "Don't do it. They'll find you and hang you. Besides, Cromwell and Lord Fairfax have almost finished this war."

"Friend Bunyan, your logic persuades me to stay. Yet you are the most foul-mouthed chap in the army."

John was always surprised when someone said that. Yet it must be true, if so many mentioned it. He made no effort to swear. Swearing was as natural as breathing.

Days after John returned to the garrison at Newport Pagnell a change was made in command. Sir Samuel Luke was mustered out, angry and sullen. The army of the Parliament was supposedly ridding itself of gentry and noblemen. Yet, some remained. So the soldiers cynically speculated it was merely one group led by Cromwell getting rid of another group.

That August John and Gibbs marched south to join a siege against the Marquis of Winchester's Basing House in Hampshire. It was proving to be the greatest fortress in England. The siege had begun in the spring of 1644. The battle was by no means one-sided either. The besieged often sallied forth unexpectedly and thrashed the attackers. One Royalist force from Oxford overpowered the attackers and took control of the nearby village of Basingstoke. They in turn were surprised and overwhelmed a few weeks later. Basing House was such a drain on the resources of Parliament that they abandoned their efforts until after the king was routed at Naseby. Now in August 1645 the siege resumed. And by September John Bunyan and Gibbs were among the besiegers.

"Well, Gibbs, this is as safe a place as any," John said upon arriving.

"Sometimes safety is an illusion."

Suddenly there was a boom, followed seconds later by an ear-shattering, bone-rattling explosion.

"What was that?" mumbled John. His ears hurt so badly he could barely hear his own voice.

"A grenade—shot by a mortar." A soldier who had been there several weeks grinned at John.

"I heard we had such violent weapons," said John. "Thank God the king's men didn't have mortars at Leicester, Gibbs."

A grenade was the newest invention of warfare. No longer did the besiegers have to rely on the dead weight of cannon balls to knock down stone walls. Now mortars lobbed a hollow iron ball full of explosives. The ball had its own fuse and exploded inside the fortress.

"But such an explosion," muttered Gibbs.

"The grenade is eighteen inches in diameter and weighs sixty-three pounds!" said the soldier. "We had to reinforce bridges all the way from London to haul that colossal mortar here to Basing House."

"What a stench," said John as the rotten-egg smell of sulfur wrenched his nose.

"It's that way all the time here," said the soldier.

"Men are going to invent their way to hell yet," grumbled Gibbs.

On October 8, Ironsides himself arrived to complete a force of 7,000 men. Now more than numbers doomed Basing House. The fatal blow would be Cromwell's iron will. On the 14th of October four cannons pummeled a wall until attackers could storm the breach. John and Gibbs were among those who stumbled through clouds of dust into the rubble of the cratered courtyards. There was no resistance. Fire raged among the buildings. Soul-rending screams came from defenders trapped in inner chambers. Their torment seemed never to end. Only 200 of the besieged remained alive to be taken prisoner.

"At least none were killed needlessly," said John unconvincingly.

When they marched back to Newport Pagnell John and Gibbs learned Cromwell had conquered Bristol in September and executed hundreds of defenders there. This was to be the course of the war for many months to come. The army of the Parliament was besieging one Royalist stronghold after another and reducing each one to rubble. Only one more battle was fought in the open, at Stowin-the-Wold in Gloucester. It was almost the king's last gasp. He fled to Scotland in May, 1646, where he was arrested.

"Friend Bunyan, Newport Pagnell is being scuttled," said a breathless Gibbs one day in August of 1646.

"I'm ready," said John.

He had been in the army for almost two years. He had been in major battles. He had been wounded. He had shot at men, although he never knew if his musket ball struck one or not. There had been grand moments in battle. But there had been many more haunting moments. He tried not to remember the dead women on the road north of Naseby. He tried not to remember the screams inside the fire at Basing House. He tried not to remember the thousands who were executed in cold blood after the battles.

"Yes, I've given my soul to the Parliament for two years," continued John. "Now I must return to Bedford to follow my father's meteoric career as a tinker."

Gibbs was worried. "Maybe not. They say Cromwell is mounting an expedition against the Irish for helping the king."

"Nothing for you to worry about, Gibbs," said their sergeant, who had drawn near. "You're being mustered out."

"You mention only Gibbs?" barked John. "Say, something is suspicious here. . . ."

"Cromwell just can't part with a young brawny lad like you, Bunyan. You've been selected to go to Chester."

"Chester?" John had to stop and think hard. Chester was very far away. It was a city on the northwest coast of England, almost in Wales. "Why, Chester is on the Irish Sea!"

53

"Bright lad too," commented the sergeant. "That's where we will embark for Ireland. . . ."

Ireland!

"It's a nasty thing to fight an Irishman on our own soil," grumbled John after the sergeant left. "But to fight him on his own soil will be. . . ." His voice trailed off in dismay.

"I've heard that since the king is out of power the Irish are murdering Englishmen living in Dublin," said Gibbs. "They think this is their chance to get us Englishmen out of Ireland once and for all."

"Where does it stop? If Cromwell subdues the Irish, do we invade Holland next? Or France?"

Soon, with dozens of other yeomen soldiers like himself and their upper-crust officers John Bunyan marched northwest though England's midlands. Northampton. Warwick. Then he tramped through counties that not long ago would have risen up against his scarlet uniform in a flash: Stafford and Cheshire. But now the counties were silent; their many castles once great were now in crumbled ruins. It was 120 miles to Chester, easy miles on a lowland between the Cambria Mountains to the southwest and the Pennines to the north. John had a lot of time to think.

John missed the older men and their wise talk, especially Gibbs. Oh, how he would miss the tough but kind presence of friend Gibbs. He would miss the tiny bookstore of Matthew Cowley in Newport Pagnell too. Gibbs had taken him there. John was amazed to hear that tracts written by men of humble situations were actually being printed and sold. The tracts savaged the established church, the Catholics, the Presbyterians, the king, the noblemen, the gentry. When had this begun? John was sure it had begun only when the king no longer tyrannized them. And so too had begun the preaching of men like Hobson against the church and the noblemen—right out in the open at Newport Pagnell, and unpunished. Cromwell himself had supposedly said, "Sir, the State in choosing men to serve it, takes no notice of their opinions, if they be faithful to it." So balanced against the atrocities of Fairfax and Cromwell were new freedoms too. But what a painful birth.

Rivers no longer flowed east but west. Rain fell more often as the marching soldiers flanked the gentle Dee River, but it was soft rain. "Get used to it," said one of the soldiers. "It rains here every other day."

"They say it never freezes here though," said another soldier optimistically.

"Good," said John. "Because winter is not far away."

In fact, John liked the looks of this gentle land. The rolling pastures along the river were greener than those to the east. The flanking hills were higher. The forests on their crowns were thicker. The cows along the river were fatter. The cottages were called magpie cottages. White plaster walls were trimmed with dark tarred wood. Yes, this was a most pleasant land. It was too bad it was no more than a stopping-off place for the voyage to Ireland.

"Chester just ahead," said their sergeant one day as they marched.

"They say Chester has a most ingenious market," said one soldier. "It is rows of shops along an elevated walkway, all covered from the damnable rain and made of timber."

"They call it 'the Rows,' " piped in another soldier.

They camped several miles outside Chester. Their sergeant said, "You men can go into Chester tomorrow.

Mind what Parliament commands you about painted women."

"Certainly," said one soldier sarcastically.

All evening the men talked of painted women or drinking ale or gambling. Much of their talk was worry over what the consequences might be if caught. It was a fact the army did not approve of men paying women for favors. But the men didn't seem concerned about whether it was right or wrong. Getting caught was the dilemma.

One soldier said, "If they catch me with a woman, are they going to discharge me or execute me?"

"Just make sure you're not caught," answered another.

But John's desire for women had died during the burial detail. Oh, how often he had thought of the women before that. But not now. Not after seeing such fair ones all mashed and thrown aside. Who was to deny that by engaging a woman, whether fair or foul, a soldier might be leading her to a similar fate? Would the king's men come by to kill her as a traitor a few weeks later?

But he went into Chester the next morning with the others. He walked "The Rows," but he could feel hostility from the shopkeepers. The seamy part of town welcomed the soldiers and their money. John even drank some ale, but stopped when he felt his spirit soaring for no good reason at all. He watched card games and eyed the women, but the dead women north of Naseby would not leave him alone. So he sought out bookshops.

"Here in Chester too are tracts deriding every aspect of English life," he blurted to the shop owner, who had read several titles to him.

"Choose your words more carefully, boy," was all the owner said.

On the way back to camp he saw two soldiers far off in a field, among some cows, talking to a shepherd. The meeting did not seem friendly. Shoving led to stalking as the two soldiers seemed to encircle the shepherd. The boy was so young he did not even know how to use his staff as a weapon. It was none of John's business. Why would he take on two of his own fellow soldiers? Probably the boy had been a fool and sassed them or praised King Charles. They would probably just give him the thrashing he deserved. And yet John stopped. The boy's frightened voice reached him. It was high-pitched. The boy must be very young. How old was Willie now? Twelve?

John reluctantly trudged across the pasture. "Hey there!" he yelled.

"What do you want?" growled one of the soldiers. "Go find your own girl."

"Girl?" And John saw the shepherd was not a young boy at all. So that was it. He saw what the soldiers were doing now. Nearby was a haystack. They were maneuvering her toward it. Any one could guess what they would do to her when hidden from view. Her voice reminded him now of his sister Margie. If any wretch had violated Margie that way, John would have strangled him in a flash. "If you harm that girl I'll see that you're both hanged," he yelled angrily. "You know that the army will do it too."

"What is your name, preacher?" asked one of the soldiers.

"Go into Chester for what you want," shouted John.

The soldiers whispered to each other, then quickly moved off toward Chester, probably hoping that John's distant glance would not be enough to identify them later.

"You had best stay closer to the farm," yelled John to the

girl. "Don't be so trusting. There are many soldiers about the countryside now."

"My master sent me out here to get the cows. He is a hard man," called the girl.

"Well, tell him we soldiers are on our way to Ireland to fight and some of us think we might not come back, so we are not so law-abiding."

"I will, good sir," she called.

"Move off," John shouted in exasperation. "Even now you are too trusting. Don't you know I could catch you before you got back to the farm?" The girl was making him so angry. She was too trusting. She did remind him of his sweet sister Margie.

"The Lord protects me," she called, "and I can tell by your voice you are not like those others."

"Oh, you foolish girl, I've seen the faces of choirboys standing over a head they just cut off!"

"You're just trying to scare me."

"No, I've seen such things."

"Have you been in many battles?"

"Listen, if you're so foolish as to stay and talk," John shouted in exasperation, "I'm going to sit down, so you will know my intentions are not to chase you."

"I know you won't, good sir. You have a profane mouth, but it is only dirt on a baby's brow."

The girl moved closer. She was trim, neither short nor tall. She was older than John thought. Perhaps sixteen, black-haired, but very fair, with rosy cheeks from the damp chill in the air. Her glossy hair was cut short and shimmered with warmth and life. Now that he saw how delicate she was, and how beautiful she was inside and out, he knew he would have fought the soldiers for her, as foolish as that would have been. The girl talked to John as if she was desperate to talk to someone. He soon found out that in spite of her youth and innocence she had problems. Her mother had been dead so long she couldn't remember her. Her father had died in the war. Her aunt's husband, an older man, had taken her in. The family was large and the girl had to work very hard.

"I'm very grateful to my aunt and uncle," she said, "but something worries me terribly. My aunt is so sickly. If the Lord takes her, I know my uncle will make me marry him. And what choice do I have?"

"Is he such a hard man?"

"He is a terrible brute." And the girl began to wring her hands.

"You must be very worried to tell me, a complete stranger."

"But you don't need to be a stranger. I'm Mary."

"And I'm John Bunyan of Elstow in the county of Bedford."

"See, we are no longer strangers, good sir."

John found himself trying to calm the girl named Mary. Her predicament pained him. Yes, he could not bear to imagine a great coarse hairy brute of an uncle trampling this beautiful fragile flower. And she was so bright. He hadn't felt such pain since he'd seen the murdered women at Naseby. It was heartbreaking. He got up, said farewell, and rushed off to camp.

If only Gibbs had been there. John could have confided in him. Where did these sharp feelings come from? Why had he rushed in to help the girl, even before he knew what a precious flower she was? But he didn't need Gibbs there to know he had to go back. Next day he ventured out into the field again, and this time he sat behind the haystack closer to the farm and out of view from the road to Chester. Would Mary come into the field? How he ached to see her. She was like an affirmation that something decent would survive the war.

Mary did come. John insisted that he sit and she keep her distance, but she did come closer to him than she had the day before. Now he could see her eyes. They were green. Mary was all obsidian and cream and emerald. He had never seen such a beautiful girl in his entire life. Of course her uncle would insist that she marry him. How could any man resist her?

"How is your aunt?" he asked anxiously.

"No better, I fear."

And they talked of what each wanted to do some day. John went back the next day. And the next. Soon they sat together but not touching. They talked on and on of what they wanted to do some day, not for a moment admitting they could ever be a "we." At night John ached for Mary.

"You know I'll soon be leaving for Ireland, don't you?" he asked her another day.

"You'll come back to England, John Bunyan," she said, then added shyly, "and you'll come to see me. Pray for my aunt's good health until then."

"Oh, I will," he answered. But then he remembered the last time he'd prayed. It had been for Margie. And the last time he'd prayed before that had been for his mother.

"Why are you looking so sour?" asked Mary.

"If there is a God in heaven, he doesn't listen to my prayers," John spoke wistfully.

"But you must have faith in Him."

"I'll remember that," he commented sourly. "I suppose

I've disappointed you."

"No. You're good inside, John, but you don't know it yet."

In camp one morning their sergeant said, "It will be a while before you men see the shops of Chester again."

"Oh no. We're sailing for Ireland," groaned one of the soldiers.

"No," said the sergeant. "It seems there are some Royalists hiding in their castles hereabouts."

"Oh no," groaned several soldiers at once.

John was stunned. He did not have time to say good-bye to Mary. He peered across the fields as he marched past her uncle's farm. She was nowhere in sight. Just as they neared the inviting town of Chester, the column turned left. The road they were on now had many army wagons moving both directions. The men marched through the village of Hawarden. Since he'd met Mary, John had desired to read his pocket Bible in the long idleness and discovered that with much effort he could read. Now he was shocked to discover he could not read the signs on the shops.

"We're in Wales," explained their sergeant.

A couple of hours later they heard the familiar booms of mortars. A great castle loomed on the horizon to the north. The sergeant told them it was Flint Castle, which had been under siege for months. That was not their destination, nor was Denbigh Castle to the southwest. No, they were going to a castle a good twenty-five miles from Chester. They were on a road that paralleled the Irish Sea, not more than four or five miles away.

They passed through a village called Holywell. A talkative soldier told them, "This is where Prince Caradoc beheaded a young maiden named Winifred because she refused his lusty desires for her. A spring gushed up right where her head fell." And John soon saw that there really was a Saint Winifred's Well. There were pilgrims there, waiting for its healing waters.

The next morning they climbed into hills and at the crest they could see the Irish Sea gleaming to the north and a river glistening below them to the west. "That is the River Clwyd," said the sergeant. "Narrow but very deep."

Ships and small boats sailed the Welsh river. John felt sick. How he hated boats. If only he knew how to swim. For some reason he did not fear a ship, but a wobbly boat made him very sick. After all, hadn't he almost drowned in the Ouse once, except for blind good luck?

"Look, there's a castle," said one of the soldiers.

John had been so concerned with the river he had not noticed. But a castle rose on their side of the river not far to the south.

"See how the west side of the castle hugs the river," said their sergeant. "Ships supplied it from the sea until we stopped them. That's our destination, men."

Men of flesh and blood against stone, thought John.

"A cold, miserable place to die," muttered one soldier, thinking the same dark thoughts. . . .

six

A Longing Heart

John studied the castle as they descended into the river valley. Most castles were on hills. This Welsh castle hugged the Clwyd, its outermost western wall brushed by the river. On the three sides unprotected by the river were a series of three walls. John could see not even the outermost wall had been breached yet. And that wall was child's play compared to the other two walls, especially the innermost. That battlement was a square that appeared to be forty feet high. If it was like the inner walls in other castles it would be ten to fifteen feet thick. Two corners of the innermost square were protected by twin thick-walled towers that enclosed a complicated and very deadly gate system. The other two corners of the square were protected by single towers. All the towers were cylindrical, so the besieged had a clear view of the outside of the innermost wall, even a good view of the second wall.

"What special death spews forth from the loopholes of those towers?" asked John to no one in particular. "Arrows? Musket balls?"

"And if you get too close," added another soldier, "you'll get a nice dose of boiling oil or molten lead."

But the sea and river that formerly supplied the castle now supplied its attackers. And huge cannons and mortars lurked to the north behind the outermost wall and blasted

63

the inner walls. The outcome was inevitable. The blocks of stone would tumble into a heap. Men would storm the breach. The castle would fall. But how many men would fall too?

"For hundreds of years Englishmen and Welshmen have been building mighty stone fortresses," said the talkative soldier that night over their campfire. "And, in a period of two or three or four years of this great war, we and Cromwell are going to destroy them all."

"Good riddance," said one soldier.

John remained silent. Somehow he was sickened by what they were doing. Yes, the talkative soldier was right. They were destroying all the castles. The king had fled. It seemed Fairfax and Cromwell were determined that no king or prince or duke or marquis or lord could ever again take refuge in a castle. Why wasn't John happy about that?

He had another reason to be unhappy. It seemed the besieged in this river castle were not negotiating. Their supplies had been cut off for weeks. Surely they were almost out of food. They were probably low on powder and balls too. So the newly arrived men from Newport Pagnell waited. A few men prayed they would not have to fight. But John didn't bother. It was pure chance whether they fought or not. It might depend on no more than the difference of one musket ball or one bushel of wheat whether or not the besieged continued to defend themselves. History was that fickle. That's why a man taking unnecessary chances with his one precious life was crazy. So why didn't he just slip away and disappear? Somehow he couldn't do that either.

"I need two men for a boat detail," said the sergeant one evening.

"Boat?" asked one soldier, who seemed forever exasperated with the stupidity of war.

"How do you think we keep Royalists from slipping up to the river wall at night and supplying the fortress?" The sergeant locked his eyes on the exasperated soldier. "I pick you. . . ."

"I can't swim."

"And who of us can?" growled the sergeant. "Are we noblemen with the time to learn such frivolous sport?" The sergeant surveyed his men. "I need someone who can fire a musket if there's trouble." His eyes stopped on John. "You, Bunyan."

So after the cloudy sky darkened to a tarry canopy John found himself stepping into a small wobbly skiff with his musket. "It's going to be a very dark night tonight. You're lucky," said the sergeant.

"No oars? No poles? I don't understand," said John.

"We have a rope stretched across the entire length of the river wall," whispered the sergeant. "It's just below the water line. All you have to do is hang on to the rope and gently pull yourselves back and forth along the wall. Naturally you must not talk. Someone could be above you on the wall. . . ."

"I'm glad it's going to be black as coal now," muttered John, and added a few choice profanities.

"Don't go too close to the far corner tower," warned the sergeant. "There's a sally port there. We have men posted close to it, but the enemy could rush down and capsize you or fire into you before our men could help you."

"How far is it across to the corner tower?" asked John's companion in exasperation.

"About two hundred feet. Lean over the side, grasp the

rope with your hands about three feet apart and slide your hands along the rope. Count each time you move the skiff three feet. Stop at sixty and listen hard. Then come back and do it all over again."

John's skin was crawling. He felt as helpless as a duck bobbing on the river with muskets trained on it from above. And that wasn't the worst of it. As he reached down into the river for the rope a chill went through his whole body. The water was icy and very deep.

The two men shuttled the skiff back and forth hour after hour. Because the water was so cold they switched at the count of thirty. Their hands softly struck the stone wall again and again. Soon their hands were numb.

Once on John's turn at the rope he realized his hands had not struck the wall for several seconds. Or were his hands so numb he could not feel stone? Yet, the rope pulled hard on his arms. "Say, is the rope getting heavy?" he whispered to the other soldier.

"They've cut it at the corner tower!" barked the exasperated soldier, not caring if anyone heard him or not.

"Pull it in as fast you can," snapped John.

And so they pulled the heavy rope as fast as they could, propelling the skiff back toward the end where they had launched it. But John had the sickening feeling they were drifting out into the river.

Suddenly he felt the skiff tipping over. "You're leaning over too far," he whispered angrily.

"So are you. Let go of the rope then."

"And drift into the sea?"

As silent and disloyal as a weasel the skiff slipped from under them. The icy water engulfed them. John grabbed hand after hand of rope, feeling the heavy line sinking deeper and deeper into the river. Soon he knew if he was going to clutch the rope he could do it only by staying under water. How far was it to the shore? He took a very deep breath. *Oh, help me, God,* he screamed inside his head. *Help me. . . .*

He spun in a black vortex of pain, sinking to the bottom of the icy river. Water scoured the inside of his head, stinging him, choking him. And it was pain in his chest that slowly brought him back to reality.

"He's breathing," said someone matter-of-factly.

"Sarge?" mumbled John. His throat was very sore.

"They must have fished the rope out by the corner tower with a pike and cut it," said the sergeant far away. "You can thank our sentry for noticing the rope go slack, Bunyan. And you can be thankful you gripped the rope like a bulldog. We pulled you in."

But John did not feel thankful at all. "I lost my musket," he muttered. "Say, where is my companion?"

"Gone. He must have lost his grip."

After that night the besiegers strung the rope about fifteen feet from the castle's river wall. The poor men in the skiff had to fight a stronger current but they were safer from getting the rope cut. Occasionally a cat-eyed sentry on the wall would see them even on the always cloudy nights and shoot at them with a musket, striking the skiff, or worse, wounding a man in the skiff. But the poor men in their patched-up skiffs kept supplies from coming into the castle at night. The few times enemy boats tried to supply the castle they were spotted by the men in their skiff. At those times, after the men had left the river, fire from cannons and muskets raked the lower part of the castle wall. So the poor vulnerable men in the wobbly skiff sped the end of the castle. And soon it fell.

When 1647 began John was bivouacked near the fallen castle. To speed the idle hours he read his pocket Bible, which was not complete but contained verses selected to instruct a soldier under headings like, "He must not fear his enemies" and, "He must consider that sometimes God's people have the worst in battle as God's enemies." They had been issued a catechism too. For over two years John had neglected it. Now he read it too.

Occasionally with a pang he remembered his plea to God for mercy in the icy river, but he convinced himself he owed no gratitude. "After all," he told himself, "the other soldier probably prayed for God's help too, and he drowned. He was unlucky. I was lucky. And that's that."

The soldiers learned the Scots had surrendered King Charles to Cromwell. The fox Cromwell had forgiven a huge debt the Scots owed England. The king was being kept under guard at Holmby House in Northampton. John waited, expecting to cross the Irish Sea and fight the "wild Irish." The soldiers' pay stopped, which had happened before. Meanwhile the army gave them pieces of paper for pay, which had not happened before.

"What is this?" complained one soldier.

John, who could read well now, answered breezily, "It's a debenture, a promise of future payment."

"Will a merchant take it as money?"

"I doubt it." Later, John asked his sergeant, "When are we returning to Chester?"

"We're waiting right here in Wales until our pay catches up with us."

Many of the soldiers began selling their debentures to officers who had real money. Of course the officers would pay only one penny for every four pence of debentures. After all, they were taking a big chance surrendering real coins for nothing but paper.

John refused to sell his. "I'm holding on to mine. We'll get paid for these soon enough, lads."

But they did not get paid. By June John was holding five months of debentures—a total of ten pounds. The officers no longer bought debentures. They were low on cash and truly worried about the piles of debentures they held. Suddenly one day the soldiers were marching back to Chester.

Their sergeant grumbled, "And still no money."

"They better not be thinking about sending me to Ireland," griped one soldier.

On the way to Chester John saw Flint Castle had been leveled. Its attackers had shown no mercy. He felt a rush of anger. Then he felt better. His own officers had not destroyed the castle hugging the River Clwyd. The soldiers had finally broken through the north wall, and as the end had neared they'd persuaded the besieged to negotiate a surrender. The attackers had taken prisoners in tow, but they had not destroyed the castle. Nor had they executed anyone.

John couldn't wait to see Mary again.

But the soldiers bivouacked too far southwest of Chester. It was several days later and only at some risk he undertook the long journey to her uncle's farm. John rushed toward the shepherd in the field.

It was not Mary! "Where is maiden Mary?" John asked a young boy.

"Cousin Mary works in the house now."

"Why?" asked John rudely.

"My mother is very ill now, scarcely rising from her bed. Say, who are you? Where are you from?"

John couldn't trust this boy with the truth. If he went back and blurted it out in front of his father, who knew what the brute would do? Maybe the brute would beat Mary. Doubt overwhelmed John. Mary seemed so distant now. Should he try to see her? He would have to go directly to the farmhouse. The brute was a Royalist. Who knew how he would react? It might result in unpleasantness, or worse. John was sure Mary's uncle now knew nothing about him. He had best leave well enough alone. It was obvious the aunt would die. And Mary would become the uncle's unwilling bride. Was that any more unfair than what he had seen for the past two and half years? Hardly.

John told the boy a lie that he had known Mary's poor deceased father and left. He trudged back to camp more dejected than he had been since Margie had died. No, this was worse. Margie's death had been God's fault. This failure was John's fault. Doubt had crushed him. And who knew what would happen yet? Ireland still awaited.

"Guess what, Bunyan?" A soldier smiled as John reached camp. Not waiting for an answer he continued, "We're all being mustered out."

"We're not going to Ireland?"

"At your own expense, if you insist on going, you blockhead," snapped another soldier.

"I couldn't afford a ride in a skiff."

"Wrong! We're being paid," grinned the first soldier.

John received ten pounds! Soon he was heading back toward Bedford in a contingent of soldiers from that area. He would have made one more attempt to see Mary but the others would not have waited and it was dangerous to travel alone. The war had been bitter. Many a Royalist would relish skewering a lone Parliamentarian. And any qualms they might have had were removed by common knowledge that many of these Parliamentarians carried several months of wages in silver coins.

"I'll just have to forget Mary," John told himself as he marched east.

"What are you muttering about, Bunyan?" asked another soldier.

"Nothing." But that lie knotted up in his stomach.

John's spirits rose as he saw Elstow again. Bunyan End looked wonderfully tranquil. The cottage warmed his heart. Willie ran out, a bright-faced lad of thirteen. John was even happy to see his father. His father didn't seem so bad now, in comparison to some of the vile men John had met in the army. A tiny grave behind the cottage jarred him. At Newport Pagnell when he first heard about his new half-brother Charles he was very angry because his father had named him after the king. But now John realized that was about the strongest form of resistance his father was capable of.

"I'm truly sorry little Charles died," he mumbled to his father and stepmother Anne.

John was tired of war and its gnawing fear. Serenity was a tonic. He even liked to tinker now. He began to understand and appreciate metals. Alloys astonished him now that he really thought about them. If he added tin to copper the alloy bronze melted much more easily than just pure copper, yet the bronze when cooled was actually harder than pure copper. If he added zinc to copper the alloy brass was easier to shape than just pure copper, yet brass was actually harder than copper. So John became serious about tinkering. But he especially liked to talk with friends at the Elstow Green.

In public he was no longer the Bunyan scamp, up to no good. Now he was the yeoman John Bunyan, traveler and soldier. And he could hold his own on almost any subject. It mattered not whether the topic was war or politics or religion. Even educated men who gathered in Elstow Green were startled by the strength of his arguments.

Of course there were detractors. "There's little sincerity in his arguments, only heat," said one of the gentry in John's hearing.

"Sour grapes," muttered John. And he continued to argue either side of a question. After all, he had heard what seemed a million arguments in the army.

The army had sharpened him another way. Many sports were played on the village green. Some were accompanied by gambling, but not so loudly that it would attract unwelcome attention. It was harder to find a better tipcat player than John Bunyan. The best tipcat players needed strength and skill and judgment. The player wielded a long bat. The "cat," a cylinder of wood two inches thick and six inches long but tapered to points on both ends, was placed on the ground. If the player did not strike the cat exactly right with the bat it would not spin straight up so he could hit it a second time, and he lost his turn with no points scored. If he hit the cat a second time he had to guess the distance in yards it traveled before hitting the ground. If the distance was less than his guess he got no points and lost his turn. If more, he received that number of points and got to bat again.

Harry played with John every Sunday afternoon. Rogers, who had lost an arm in the war, studied the onlookers.

Eventually some dandy from Bedford or traveler off the High Road would stroll in, stop to see big bland-faced John Bunyan whacking the cat and comment, "That foul-mouthed redheaded bloke is pretty good."

"Thinks he is," countered Rogers dryly. "But his game changes if money is bet."

John's game did change. With money on the line, his first stroke popped the cat higher so he could take a full swing with wrists snapping the bat in perfect timing. The cat blurred into the distance, and John never overestimated the distance. An hour or two later John would have the visitor's money—fair and square. He would then split the money with his two accomplices. His victims rarely complained. After all, who wanted to admit they had been thrashed by a backward tinker from Elstow?

John's serious tinkering and just as serious gambling actually added to the nest egg he had brought back from Chester. But his life seemed empty.

It was some months before he faced the truth: he had let Mary down. "You'll come back, John Bunyan," she had said, "and you'll come to see me." But he hadn't. He had been afraid.

During the day he could forget her, but not at night. He had seen all the young ladies of Elstow. None could compare to Mary. Some were as pretty. Some were as shapely. Some were as intelligent. Some were as pure. Some were as fun to talk to. But not one combined all these qualities as Mary did. He knew that now. What if her aunt still lived? What if by pure luck her aunt fully recovered? What if her uncle was arranging a marriage for Mary right at this very moment? What a fool John would have been. Summer was the only safe time for a young woman to travel on foot.

"Next summer I will surely go and bring Mary back," he told himself.

The news that King Charles had escaped Cromwell's soldiers during the winter of 1647 and 1648 shocked John. Amazingly, the king formed an alliance with the Scots who had already betrayed him once. And the king could rely on help from the always pugnacious Irish. Now when summer came John could not go into Royalist country after Mary. The resurgence of the Royalists made that too dangerous. John tried to console himself by visiting the dimlit fields around Elstow during May Day, but he left untainted. No woman of the night could compete with the memory of Mary. In August, Cromwell's army smashed King Charles and his Scottish allies. But by the time John heard that good news it was too late in the summer to accomplish what he had to do.

"Next summer I will surely go and bring Mary back," he told himself, remembering he had used those same words before.

And so time passed, with John tinkering, playing the dashing bachelor in the village green and agonizing over Mary at night. That winter Cromwell and his cronies made one last effort to negotiate an arrangement with the imprisoned King Charles, whereby he would be a figurehead of a king and let Parliament rule. The king was intractable. In January 1649 he was beheaded. John was saddened by the death of King Charles. But he was heartened by the unchallenged rule of Oliver Cromwell.

"Next summer will surely be different. I'll go to Mary," John told himself. Then he added, "If I'm lucky."

Next May Day was a festive time, as always. It was an

excellent time to travel the countryside. Many people were traveling to celebrations and fairs. Strangers were not that noticeable. His father was surprised when in April John said he would be traveling for a while. But he raised no objection and asked no questions. John was a man now. His father prayed that God bless and protect him. John felt guilty. His father seemed to hold nothing against him, even though John had defied him in so many ways. It didn't make sense. But he was too excited to ponder the question. At last he was going after Mary.

"This summer I will surely bring Mary back," he told himself. "I will stop at nothing."

John retraced his steps of nearly two years before. He was twenty years old now. Several times he was stopped by hostile questioners. But he knew how to slip back and forth from side to side, as surely as he knew how to argue both sides of any topic. If a nobleman stopped him, John was clever enough to find out if he had been an officer with Cromwell or a cavalier for the king. If the latter, John assured him he had fought for King Charles under Sir Jacob Astley—the king's commander of the infantry himself. And John knew enough to ward off any further questions. If the inquisitor was a Parliamentarian, John's defense was easy enough. Telling the truth was easy— maybe even easier than lying.

One bright afternoon he saw green pastures he had thought about ever since he left Elstow. He hid his knapsack under a haystack. This time John stalked the shepherd, lying up behind hedges and shrubs and haystacks. Sure enough, it was Mary's cousin. John waited until the boy took the cows in and followed a safe distance behind. The white farmhouse was typical magpie, so cheerfully

75

white in black trim it didn't seem possible the aunt could still be dying inside. John's heart sank. Near the farm yard, a scrawny dog, more bark than body, detected him.

"Say, who are you?" demanded the surprised boy. "Where are you from?"

"I'm a traveler," answered John civilly. Barking dogs swarmed all around his legs. In seconds his indifference calmed them. A wandering tinker felt no fear or hostility for a mere dog. "May I drink from your well, lad?"

"Why did you leave the road?" The boy nodded toward the south.

"Oh, I don't come from that direction at all. I come from a farm to the northeast. I crossed the countryside from Helsby Hill. Surely you've heard of that grand precipice, haven't you, lad?" The lies flowed from John. Of course he felt as if he really did know every town and creek and hill in the neighborhood. After all, Mary had told him and he knew now he had forgotten not one word she'd ever said.

"I'll ask my father," said the boy suspiciously, and ran inside the farmhouse.

Soon a huge brute rushed out. . . .

seven

A Journey of Love

"What do you want?" snarled the brute in a voice that tried to please no one. He was worse than John had imagined. His eyes were cunning pig's eyes in folds of fat. He was hairy enough to play the ape at a fair.

"Only a drink, sir. I'm from the environs near Helsby Hill. On my way to Chester." John felt sick. Fooling the boy was one thing. Fooling this brute, who probably knew the area around Helsby Hill like the palm of his hand, was not going to be easy.

"Been to the Peckforth Hills lately?" asked the brute slyly.

"To see Beeston Castle?" countered John easily.

"Do you know a wee farmer over by Helsby Hill named William Grady?" queried the brute.

"William Grady?" mulled John. His mind was reeling. How should he answer? Suppose the brute had just invented William Grady?

The door to the house burst open. A figure came flying out in blouse and skirt. "I'll get the stranger a drink." It was Mary!

"Who told you to come out here, woman?" snarled the uncle. His piggy eyes raked her. "Make it quick then," he grunted. But as Mary visited their well she kept a constant chatter which seemed to throw her uncle off stride. He tried to get back to his searching questions, yet intercepted her every comment so that John could not talk with her. John could scarcely think anyway, seeing Mary more beautiful, more womanly than before. And he had never known she was so clever.

After Mary returned with a dipper of water John took it from her, and as he pretended to drink he whispered, "How is your aunt?"

"The sky is peculiar today," Mary said with a frown. "It seems as if winter could come at any moment."

So the aunt was just barely alive, thought John, as the uncle loudly disagreed with Mary's comment about the weather. John noticed the uncle scowling at him. "Well, I had best get going to Chester," said John. "I'm going to marry soon if all works out. I expect I'll know sometime after dark."

"Do you think we're interested in your life story, you red-headed oaf?" growled the uncle. "Get on your way and don't stop here on your way back."

"Surely, sir."

John strode quickly out of the farmyard. He walked briskly across the field. *Oh, please God, let Mary under-stand me and come tonight.* And he realized he had prayed for the first time in a long time. It had just slipped out. He burrowed into a haystack and waited for dark. He was very depressed now. His prayers had never been answered. Or had they? Hadn't he prayed for help when the skiff cap-sized at the river castle? But what about his companion who had died? Doubt was so tiresome.

"Oh, what's the harm? Please, God, deliver Mary to me tonight."

It dimmed to a typical night for those cloudy parts. It was tarry black. If Mary came, would she see him? He left the stack and walked farther into the field. He mustn't get too close to the farmhouse and alarm the dogs. He rested against a haystack and every few seconds whistled softly in a pitch so low it was barely distinguishable from the wind or a lovesick owl. After a while his mouth was dry as paper.

"Is that you, John Bunyan?"

"Mary!"

They stood distant from each other, almost as if they were denying their former feelings. But slowly they approached each other.

"I never stopped hoping," said Mary. Her voice carried tears of joy.

"I wish I could have courted you properly," said John.

"Thank the Lord you didn't try. As it is, my uncle doesn't know who you are or where you are from."

"Come with me, Mary. As my wife, of course."

"But the church won't marry me here or anywhere without asking questions."

"A justice of the peace can marry us in this new era of Cromwell. The law has changed, Mary." John waited, his heart in his mouth. Was it possible she didn't want to go with him?

"I have no dowry. I don't remember ever touching a coin. I am poorer than I was the day I was born."

"You yourself are a great treasure to me."

"Let me pray a moment," she asked.

John waited in silence. Why did she have to pray? What could she possibly learn kneeling in a pasture under a black-clouded sky? God was more remote, more invisible

79

than the stars. Maybe even that comparison was too weak. John knew stars existed above the shroud of clouds. But did God?

"I must go back," she said finally.

"No!" cried John. He had heard the same pain from a man hit by a musket ball.

". . .to get my clothing and a few other things."

So God had answered her. But how? He must remember to ask her sometime. As he waited his fears mounted. What if the brute stopped her? John had seen many heartbreaking injustices in this world. How many soldiers died by moving one inch this way or one inch that way, or by moving one second too soon or one second too late? Why did he let her go back? Time crawled across his skin like a spider.

"John?"

"Mary!"

She handed John her things bundled inside a sheet. John retrieved his knapsack from under the haystack. Hand in hand they found the rough road and scurried to the southeast in darkness.

"We'll have to hide during the day," said John. "Just before I got here I bought several loaves of bread and a block of cheese, so we will not have to stop to buy food and leave a trail. We'll make it, Mary. I just know it."

Mary asked no questions. It was too obvious they had to remain hidden during the day. Her uncle would pursue them for a few days at least. Just before dawn they crawled deep into a haystack to wait out the day. It was too warm in their makeshift nest but they whiled away the hours whispering about the future. Mary's breath bathed him in milk and honey and promises. Eventually they slept a while in the prickly heat and left their haven after it got dark. The night air struck them like buckets of cold water. In a creek they drank and washed off before they continued southeast. After several days of traveling only at night they emerged to travel during the day. John's timing had been perfect. Many people were traveling about the countryside for the May Day fairs.

In Newport Pagnell John's old army friend Gibbs, now pastor of a nonconformist church there, took John and Mary to a Justice of the Peace. The newlyweds stayed with Pastor Gibbs for two days, scarcely noticed in the May Day celebration. John would never doubt again his decision to go back for Mary. Bliss, ecstasy, enchantment, fulfillment. Mary exhausted his power of thought.

From Newport Pagnell they went on east through Huntingdon. From there they circled back to arrive at Bunyan End from the northeast.

"Mary, is it?" asked his father, his face full of wonder, after John introduced her as his wife.

"From these here parts, Mary?" asked John's stepmother Anne.

"Mary is from a farm near the sea," said John, then deftly made that truth into a lie. "Didn't you see us come from the northeast?"

"Oh, from the fens, no doubt," enthused Anne. "I've heard of that miraculous land being rescued from the watery world of eels and crabs. And what is your last name, dear?"

"Why, it is Bunyan," laughed John.

No one in Elstow or Bedford would ever know Mary's maiden name. The stepmother never had a chance to pry because John soon rented a small cottage right on the main street of Elstow. He would build a forge in back. The couple owned almost nothing, but John had a nest egg and Mary revealed she had brought more in her bundle than she had admitted: she had two books.

Even though John had learned a lot about bookmakers and books in the army he still was amazed that common people like himself could own books. And here was Mary, the poorest of the poor, with not one book, but two.

"My father left me these," she said proudly. "He was a very Godly man."

John might have argued that point if Mary herself wasn't such glowing proof. "And what are these books?"

"*The Practice of Piety* by Bishop Lewis Bayly and *The Plain Man's Pathway to Heaven* by Pastor Arthur Dent."

John began to read the books with Mary, more to show off his skill at reading than because of any interest in the subject matter. Bishop Bayly's book told him grace is abundant for sinners if they repent, a fact that he found pleasant but irrelevant. It scarcely applied to him. Bayly believed few rich people would be saved. John found that belief to his liking. Bayly was pleasant enough to read. And John found that Mary read it very well too. Something in it seemed to disturb Mary a little, but John didn't know what.

Her second book *The Plain Man's Pathway to Heaven* by a preacher, Arthur Dent, took John's imagination by storm. It agreed in many ways with the book by Bayly, especially the difficulties of being both rich and virtuous. But it was so much more a story. It was about four characters who sat down under an oak tree during May Day to have a lively conversation.

One of the characters was Antilegon, a cavalier, who

commended merriment as a goal in itself. And his cynical views on life were none other than those John had heard expressed by many Ranters! Antilegon scoffed at everything. Another character, Philagathas, was an honest layman. Another, Asunetos, represented an ignorant fool and a fourth, Theologus, the theologian. The conversation was witty. Often their comments revealed that what one promoted as a virtue—like hospitality—could actually be perverted into a vice—like gluttony.

"What a wonderful and witty way to explain things," John told Mary. "And they are written so simple and plain, in English the people speak. At first I thought I had never encountered anything like it before, it was so entertaining. But now I remember a couple of such books the soldiers read aloud for entertainment in the garrison at Newport Pagnell. One book had delightful conversations among characters named Sir Worldly Wise and such. And another book had characters named Persecution, Reason, and Conformity, who were tried before a judge named God's-vengeance and a jury of Liberty, Innocence, Gospel. . . ."

"The Gospel!" interrupted Mary. "That is the wisdom a man needs to be Godly—like my father."

"Are you going to tell me again how he meddled in the affairs of everyone, correcting them of every vice?"

"Go with me to church, John. Listen for yourself."

"I've been to church a thousand times," said John. "It was the law of England. Remember? It's no longer the law."

"I have no way to go to church unless you take me."

Enthused by *The Plain Man's Pathway to Heaven* John went on to tell Mary the stories that had been read at the garrison. He marveled that he could remember the stories so well. "It's been four years since I last heard those stories, yet I remember all of each story, even all the names."

"It's the use of clever names that bonds the story to your memory," ventured Mary.

"Yes, you're right. That's the device that makes it stick, of course. I see it now. As much as I like Pastor Dent's book, his names—Theologus, Asunetos and so forth—irritate me in their strangeness. They must be Greek or Latin."

"I believe they have the ring of Latin," said Mary. "That cadence rings in my ears from church. I miss church terribly. Won't you take me to church, John?"

John did not think of himself as a hard man, and Mary's green eyes could melt his heart. It wasn't long before John was escorting Mary to church in Elstow. John found he did not mind. He paid little attention to the sermons of the pastor, Christopher Hall. What he enjoyed was the finery of church. The church was the most opulent experience of his life. He began to hunger for it. With Mary's help he learned every jot and tittle of the pastor's vestments, even the cloth of the bishop: the long flowing alb, the long stole over the alb, the tunicle over that—right on up to the amice around his neck and to his crowning miter. John admired the fine vestments of the pastor's helpers as well. Maybe he could wear such finery some day. He began taking Mary twice a day, morning and evening. And it paid off. It wasn't long before the pastor allowed John to ring the bells before each service.

"What joy!" he told Mary after each service. "To think it is poor me, hanging from the ropes, pealing those magnificent bells. I can feel the vibrations pass right down from my clutched hands to my toes."

At first John had admired the five huge bells in the bell

tower through the eyes of a tinker. They were a specific mix of bronze called bell metal which could be easily melted and cast in huge clay molds. But after a while John began to appreciate the harmony of the bells, then to actually long for it. He seemed to have an innate sense of music. Hours after he rang them, the tenor, the treble, the alphabet, and the other bells still harmonized inside his head. Then to be able to return to the tower and actually ring them again himself seemed too good to be true.

With Mary, John's life was very different from before. He seemed to be almost respected now. Oh, he still played in the village green every Sunday. He still swore, some people said, although he never remembered doing it. But his life had undergone many changes. One of the biggest changes came in late fall of 1649. Mary was going to have a baby!

"I had doubts renting such a fine cottage, with a loft and all," gushed John, "but now I see it is a good thing."

"Perhaps God nudged you."

"Perhaps," said John, unconvinced.

One Sunday in church John stopped admiring Pastor Hall's vestments long enough to hear the pastor railing against men who worked or played games on Sunday. John was stunned. That applied to him. What could possibly be wrong with tipcat? He and his friends no longer bet. John considered that new development a virtue, although there was no one around who would bet him anymore. His skill was too well known. Still, he wasn't betting, was he? He deserved some credit, didn't he? He managed to put the sermon out of his mind. It was a good thing he rarely listened.

That afternoon in the village green John took his first

stroke at tipcat, spinning the cat off the ground into the air. It looked as big as a melon. John stopped the bat in a huge backswing. He would swing his shoulders around, snap his wrists, and surely he would hit it a mile.

A voice pummeled him, "Will you leave your sins and go to heaven, or have your sins and go to hell?"

John dropped his bat. Who was that? He looked into the sky. Suddenly he felt terrible guilt. What he was doing was wrong. He felt sick. He had never felt so miserable. He looked at Harry and Rogers. They looked at him strangely.

"Did you hear that?" he asked them.

"I heard only the cat drop to the ground without you hitting it," sneered Harry. "Move out of the way. It's my turn."

While Harry took his turn at bat John's head was swimming. Never had he felt such guilt. But what could be done now to change anything? Surely he was lost. The voice that condemned him surely damned him too. When John's turn came again he decided to play on. What could he do about his sinning now? If he was lost, he was lost. He might as well sin. With a mighty swing he stroked the cat into the sky.

But that afternoon he went home knowing for the first time in his life he was a sinner. He really knew it. God or an angel had told him. Later that week he was talking with Harry outside the shop of an older woman, who didn't have the best reputation in Elstow. Suddenly she rushed out of the shop and faced him.

"You make me tremble, John Bunyan," she said. "I never heard such a man for swearing."

"Me?" asked John incredulously.

"You're the most ungodly man in Elstow. I pray the

young boys don't fancy you and take after you."

After she went inside the shop John said to Harry, "What brought that on?"

"Pay no attention to her. She has no room to lecture anyone. Suppose you do swear every other word, so what?"

But it bothered John very much. He felt as if he had been slapped. Was his tongue so foul it even shocked such a tainted woman? He was sure he didn't talk much worse than his father. But maybe he had picked up a few more curses in the army. Did all those people he thought he impressed so much in the village green really think he was a coarse, foul-mouthed fool? Was he, John Bunyan, nothing more than the ignorant fool Asunetos? He felt tremendous shame. *God in heaven*, thought John, *if only I could be a child again and learn how to speak like the godly.*

"Please, God. Help me shed this terrible burden of my foul mouth."

That night at supper he talked a great deal trying to shake his feeling of shame and noticed Mary looking at him in wonder. "What's wrong?" he asked sheepishly. He felt rotten. Was he cursing that very moment and not knowing it? "Did I just say something wrong?"

Mary had tears in her eyes. "You haven't said one oath the entire meal. Not so much as one."

"Is that so unusual?"

"Have some more carrot soup, dear." Her green eyes were wide with admiration.

After dinner they read the Bible together. Nothing John had bought for Mary pleased her so much as this new kind of Bible common folks were buying. Cromwell himself had commissioned it. John found himself now reading this Bible eagerly. No wonder his friend Gibbs had cherished it. It had magnificent stories. And for some reason John wanted to believe with all his heart and soul it was truly God speaking. Yes, the Ten Commandments were astonishing, truly wonderful instructions for being Godly. But were they from the heart of God? Or were they from the head of Moses?

One night when Mary was large but still long before the baby was due she started having rhythmic pains. Mary would not admit what the pains meant. But John saw terror cloud her green eyes. Birth now would be a disaster. She writhed beside John in agony, moaning, trying to pretend the waves of pain meant nothing. His Mary in pain was the worst thing John could imagine. Silently he prayed, *Lord, if you will now remove this labor from my wife and cause her no more trouble this night, then I will know for sure you can discern the most secret thoughts of the heart.* In an instant Mary stopped moaning and fell into a deep sleep.

Yet the next day John doubted. "It was so miraculous," he told himself. "Was I dreaming?"

Mary had no more pain until many weeks later when in July of 1650 she went into much desired labor. John's stepmother Anne came to attend to Mary while his father calmed John. The birth was long and difficult. Hours later John looked in awe at Mary holding their tight-fisted, apricot-faced baby daughter swaddled in a blanket. The new parents baptized the daughter and christened her Mary. But John's joy evaporated as they realized baby Mary was either blind or severely retarded.

"Why?" John asked himself. Why, when everything was going so smoothly, had this happened? And hadn't he even reformed? Wasn't he trying to keep the Ten Commandments? And when he did occasionally break one, didn't he afterwards repent and ask for forgiveness? Why would God treat His new creatures John and daughter Mary so rudely? Perhaps John had not reformed. He thought about it. Had he tempted God that night when Mary had gone into labor too soon? Was that it? Or was it his doubt that God had answered his prayer that night? Or was it something he was still doing? Yes, he was still dancing. Just this last May Day, with Mary sitting huge with child, he had danced around the May Pole for hours and enjoyed every moment of it. And then there were the bells at church. How he loved not only to ring them, but be acknowledged as the one who rang them.

So he gave up dancing and ringing bells.

He still lingered in the bell tower before every service, bathing himself in the glory of the pealing bells. But after a few times of this he could not stop thinking about his poor daughter Mary, whom he now knew was blind. She was so helpless. What if a bell came loose from above and came crashing down? John had been in war. He had seen men freshly crushed, still crawling and groping for a few minutes like stubborn smashed insects. He knew what his last thoughts would be: *My poor Marys. How I let them down.* So John began to back into an archway between the tower and the church to listen to the bells. Then he imagined a bell breaking loose during its swing. It would fall not straight down but at an angle, ricocheting off a wall and smashing John. So he began to back off all the way to the door into the church to listen to the bells. But what good would that do if the entire tower collapsed? Finally John delayed leaving for church until he actually heard the bells beckon him like everyone else in Elstow. By the time

89

he reached church the ringing of the bells had ceased. So he completely gave up bell ringing as well as dancing.

Just how far he had come was borne out a few days later. On the street he met old friend Harry. "How have you been, Harry?" he asked sheepishly because the truth was he had been avoiding Harry for several weeks as if Harry were the cause of his former sinful ways.

"Oh, very well, Bishop Bunyan," Harry answered sarcastically, adding a string of profanities about God and the church.

"Harry, what if you should die separated from God?"

"What would the devil do for company without the likes of me?" sneered Harry. And, cursing John, he walked away.

eight

A Journey of Faith

*J*ohn was stunned by Harry.
Harry was exactly as John had once been. He had no sense of sin at all. Sin was no more than a joke to Harry. How righteous John felt now. He had even mastered the essential historical facts in the Bible, although much of the books by Saint John and Saint Paul mystified him.

I'm a godly man now, he reassured himself.

Weeks later on a sunny fall day John was in Bedford, soliciting business by trudging the back streets, chanting "Tinker, tinker." He came upon several women sitting in front of a cottage, apparently wives and daughters of common tradesmen like himself. To his pleasure they were talking about God. John was always a brisk talker and this seemed a good opportunity to impress these women in the hope they had a metal pot or two to mend.

"Good morning, ladies. I hear mention of God."

"Join our fellowship, friend," answered one of the women. And she went on to talk about being born again.

John waited for an opportune time to break in and take over the conversation. But the time never came. The women spoke like no common people he had ever heard. Only his wife Mary came close to sounding so holy. The women spoke of how God was in their hearts, but also how

91

wretched they still were in their sin. They confessed a great love for Jesus and each one related how Jesus had enabled her to fight off the devil's temptations. John was amazed, not only by the ease and naturalness with which they articulated their love for Christ, but by the joy in their faces. These common women were radiant and spoke with more eloquence and conviction than the pastor. They were not common at all, but beautiful and special in a holy way. John now realized he knew nothing about being reborn. He had never found the joy in the Bible these women found. His sense of sin was not nearly as powerful as theirs.

"Excuse me, ladies, I must take my leave," he finally muttered. Once again he felt like the ignorant fool Asunetos.

John hurried home to read the Bible with Mary. Over the next months he read the Bible eagerly. He felt blessed when the infant Mary showed signs of being very intelligent, although blind. He found himself going back to those same women in Bedford again and again. He was tempted less and less to talk briskly. He tried always to back his opinion with Scripture now. And he listened and asked questions. From them he gained a sense of the continual presence of God. Every decision he made now was for God's approval. And he gained a profound respect for the Bible. It had elevated these common women to the level of bishops. And it had elevated him too. He was now understanding Saint Paul. Now John knew his own righteous behavior, admirable as it was, would not save his soul. Salvation was a gift from Christ. All John had to do was believe that. He just had to have faith. Salvation would follow.

Yet John agonized whether or not he had faith. Did he really believe? He still talked to people like Harry who didn't believe at all, or to people who had "educated" themselves into Ranters. The Ranters especially caused John to doubt. He was drawn again and again to the women in Bedford, and every time they dissolved his doubt.

One day following a hard rain, as he walked to Bedford, he wondered if his faith could be proven by a miracle. After all, didn't Christ say in the Bible that if a man had enough faith he could move a mountain? If John had faith then why couldn't he perform a small miracle? What if he commanded the puddles in the road to become dry? Wouldn't that prove he had faith? But just as suddenly he was overwhelmed with doubt. How could he handle the failure if he couldn't work a miracle? It would mean his certain doom! So he continued on to Bedford deeply depressed.

That same day John found the women gathered as usual and asked, "Ladies, I know your wisdom springs from the Bible, but who first ministered such wisdom to you?"

"From our Pastor Gifford. We go to his Free Church of Bedford."

A few days later, whether John had a vision or a daydream he wasn't sure. What he saw were the Bedford women on the side of a mountain basking in the sun. He himself stood in snow, shivering under black clouds. A wall encircled the mountain. He began to search the wall intently for some passage, so he could join the women. Finally he found a doorway to a passage, very straight and narrow. It took many hours just to squeeze his head into the doorway, but eventually he wriggled his entire body inside the door. Then he squirmed and wriggled through the passage. Once inside he climbed the side of the mountain to join the women in radiant sunshine.

"Mary," he said later, "next Sunday we're going to the Free Church in Bedford."

So John began taking Mary to the Free Church in Bedford. Its official membership was little more than its twelve founders. It had existed only since 1650. Under the king such a church would never have been tolerated. Its young pastor, John Gifford, became John Bunyan's tutor. Once in a private conversation in which John had confessed his torment Pastor Gifford interrupted him to confess that he had been in the king's army.

"A Royalist!" exclaimed John.

"Yes. And I tell you only so you will see my own tortuous path to Christ. It's best in these ebbs and flows of kings and noblemen to be mute on your war service. What may be considered your virtue one year will be your death warrant the next year."

"I'll surely remember that, Pastor Gifford. But how was your path so tortuous?"

"I tell you truthfully, John, it has not been more than four years ago I fought against Lord Fairfax just southeast of London at Maidstone."

"Is there any ground in England not soaked with blood?"

"I was a major. . . ."

"A major!"

"Yes. My reward for that exalted rank and my particular stubbornness was the sentence of death after we surrendered."

"Death!"

"Yes. Fairfax picked me and eleven others to set an example."

"But you're here. . . ."

"My escape was as miraculous to me as Peter's escape in the book of Acts."

John quoted from memory: " 'And, behold, the angel of

the Lord came upon him, and a light shined in the prison: and he smote Peter on the side, and raised him up, saying, Arise up quickly. And his chains fell off from his hands. And the angel said unto him, Gird thyself, and bind on thy sandals. And so he did. And he saith unto him, Cast thy garment about thee, and follow me. And he went out, and followed him; and wist not that it was true which was done by the angel; but thought he saw a vision.' "

"What a memory you have for Scripture, John. It must be a gift given you by God for some great purpose."

"But how did you escape, pastor?"

"It was my sister who came to see me in prison. She told me all the guards were either drunk or asleep. I felt like Peter. As if I were in a dream. With my sister I simply walked right out of prison. I hid in the fields in the days and I crept north at night—all the way to Bedford. God saved me for sure, John. But this next part is the reason I tell you all this. I practiced medicine in my new life in Bedford. But was I thankful to God? Hardly. I drank and gambled and cursed. One night I lost a great amount of money gambling and fell into a rage, cursing God for my bad luck. But abruptly I was overwhelmed by a sense of sin. Suddenly I saw how vile I had become. I fell to my knees. Once a man seeks God, John, God will find him."

John stared at this saintly man. "What an astonishing transformation. Your journey to God is more remarkable than mine."

"Your journey is far from over," answered Pastor Gifford.

He gave Martin Luther's *Comments on Galatians* to John to read. Amazingly, Luther described his own torment. So John was not alone. The pastor had suffered torment. Even the great Luther himself had suffered such doubts. But after a while, instead of being consoled, John was tormented again. Yes, the pastor and a great man like Luther could withstand the devil. But how could he, John Bunyan?

So even with encouragement from Luther and his own good shepherd, Pastor Gifford, John remained in torment. One day in a moment of exasperation he thought, *Oh, let Christ go.* Immediately he began to worry. How rash he had been! Had he, like Esau, given up his birthright? For weeks John alternated between belief he was saved and belief he was damned.

By 1652 Mary was going to have another baby. Neither she nor John should have worried. Worry showed a lack of trust in God. But John did worry.

When the baby was stillborn, John was crushed. First, a blind child, next a dead child. Was this God's judgment on him? Maybe John was not one of the "elect," those souls chosen by God to be saved from the beginning of creation. It didn't matter what he did. He would never be saved.

John continued to wallow in doubt. Many things around him seemed evidence that most people fell to the devil. He saw old people still grasping after material things. How could they be so foolish? Pious people grieved the dead with much wailing. If they were certain the dead person was in paradise, why would they be in such obvious sorrow? This latter observation jarred him. He had felt the same way when he'd grieved his lost child.

"Surely I'm being deceived by the devil!" he told himself. "I must have faith."

He was in such torment he hardly realized and little cared what was happening in England. Parliament's long bloodbath against the Royalists, against the Irish, and against the Scots was over. Now the English fought the Dutch in great sea battles. Oliver Cromwell, backed by his soldiers, had dissolved Parliament. He named himself Lord Protector and created a new constitution.

"Good Lord, he's made himself the new king!" said some.

"He simply wants to provide stable government and to tolerate all the Puritan sects," said others. "He refuses the title of king."

"He is allowing Jews in the country for the first time in over three hundred years," said some in worry.

"Surely that is a measure of his toleration of all religions," answered others.

Even John in his torment sensed the great toleration that pervaded England. He never considered Oliver Cromwell evil. Of course, Parliament's armies during the war had committed terrible atrocities. To his dying day John would never forget those poor crushed women at Naseby. But was Oliver Cromwell responsible? Wasn't Lord Fairfax the ranking general at that time? Besides, the bloody war was now remembered as the "Civil War."

About this time John's perseverance paid off. Faith, hope, and love crystallized. He had not doomed himself like Esau. It had just been the devil tempting him to give up hope. As far as the dead were concerned, John had almost let something that from God's perspective was blessed and just steal his faith. The dead should be mourned because they will be sorely missed, but they should not be regarded as lost. But how had he regained his virtues? He realized it had happened, not through his great power of reasoning, or even his perseverance, but through the mystery of God's grace. Praise God.

As for his blind daughter he was wrong to lament that

too. She was so dear to him he couldn't imagine loving any child more. And she herself could not have been more loved by two parents. Was she such a tragedy? Every night, undistracted by the sight of pretty baubles of no consequence, she listened intently to the Bible and the talk that followed. So, at the age of two she was talking as brightly as a child of five.

"She knows at two what I didn't know at twenty!" John exclaimed.

John continued tinkering, but helped Pastor Gifford more and more. In 1653, John applied to become the nineteenth member of the Free Church, just about the time they were allowed to have their services in the ancient chapel of St. John's. The Free Church required new members to openly bare their souls. Any candidate for membership had to give the congregation an account of the work of grace in their soul. John was trembling, but spoke for a long time.

After the service Pastor Gifford said, "Your account was full indeed."

Other members came to him.

"Well spoken, Brother Bunyan."

"I was moved, Brother Bunyan."

"I never heard rebirth detailed in such a passionate way," enthused another. "What torment you have endured."

"It seems you have some gift for expressing yourself," said Pastor Gifford.

"Which I use only as a stalking horse for material things," said John humbly.

"Not today," said Pastor Gifford. "Today you speak for Christ."

John had felt guilty for some time about his talent for talking glibly about anything under the sun and equally well on every side of it. But now he realized the pastor was right. Speaking well was a gift—which could be used for good or evil or matters of no importance at all. Today he had used it for the ultimate good: Christ. He had an astonishing thought: Was it possible a mere tinker like himself might someday speak for Christ every day? And what about the doubts that always came back to haunt him?

"John, I'm going to have a baby," said Mary one evening in the fall of 1653.

It was tempting to make the next birth a test again of God's blessing on the Bunyans. But John fought the temptation. The devil tried to make every event in a man's life a sign of whether God approved or disapproved, whether God loved or was distant, or even whether God existed or did not exist at all.

On April 14, 1654, Mary gave birth to Elizabeth. Betsie, as they called her, was tiny but normal in every respect. And John's inner life became more stable. He had to constantly remind himself the healthy baby was not an omen for him or Mary. Healthy Betsie had her own life and being and purpose, according to God's will, not his own.

John was now very active in the church, accompanying Pastor Gifford or one of the brothers in counseling or in reprimanding or in consoling or in a hundred other things. Occasionally John himself spoke to a brother or sister. In his own mind he spoke so weakly that for the first time he began to doubt his speaking anything of real value, even though those present said he was effective.

John was spending so much time in Bedford now that in 1655 he and Mary decided to move there. That spring John developed a severe illness in his lungs and was so wracked with coughing he became weaker and weaker. Worst of all he once again succumbed to doubt. Inside he cried, *Are these the fruits of Christianity? Are these the tokens of a blessed man?* He was further sickened by his own doubts. And his sickness furthered his doubts.

"Will doubts ever cease?" he cried in their small cottage.

John gradually regained his health, finally so much so that his doubts seemed self-pity. They appeared especially selfish when he learned Pastor Gifford was very sick. It was at this time John was asked to help out by preaching in church. This brought him to his knees. How could he do it? Once he would have preached briskly, but now he felt very weak and undeserving. But he remembered Saint Paul's words in First Corinthians: "they have addicted themselves to the ministry of the saints. . .submit yourselves unto such. . ."

So John agreed to preach. Pastor Gifford counseled him from his sickbed. John must write his sermon very carefully beforehand. That way he could arrange his thoughts in a very convincing way. And, the pastor advised him that if someone as bright as his wife Mary could not understand what John wrote then surely no one would understand it when he spoke it in church. Besides, John would have a record of the sermon and be able to use it again. John was sure he would never preach a second time, but he wrote and rewrote his sermon. When Mary could not understand a certain part he revised it until she did understand. He came to realize with certainty that it was not Mary's lack of reasoning that made some of his assertions unintelligible but the way he put the words together. He gave that problem a lot of thought.

I must express myself so that my view is as clear as morning dew.

Finally John delivered his sermon. In spite of his thorough preparation he was nauseated. He told the congregation he preached to them in chains. He was a sinner himself and if he knew anything at all he knew they had to recognize their own sin before they could repent. Without a conviction of sin no one could be saved. And without being saved, the soul was damned to an eternity of hellfire!

After he preached, Mary congratulated him, then whispered, "Were you frightened?"

"Sick at first. Weak-kneed. But afterwards, soaring into the heights. What fright before! What vain glory after! It is hard to know whether I am more despicable before I preach or more despicable afterwards."

But the brothers and sisters thanked him and insisted he moved them to contemplate their sin very mightily. He did not know them to lie just to be polite. So maybe he could preach passably after all. So he agreed to preach when they needed him. His torment for so many years had forced him to digest the Bible from Genesis to Revelation. And he found that he could pull up Scripture at will while he prepared a sermon.

In September of 1655 it was John Bunyan who addressed the congregation after the sermon. "Brothers and sisters, I read you this letter from Pastor Gifford. It is addressed, 'To the church over which God made me an Overseer when I was in the world.'" John went on to read the heartbreaking but wise letter from the deathbed of Pastor Gifford.

Later, John confided in Mary, "I hope others don't think I'm cold because I don't grieve from the rooftops, but faith in Christ forces me to believe Pastor Gifford is better off than we who remain."

"It's best to use our grief to comfort his poor wife and

101

four children."

"Yes, the church must care for its widows."

It was not until January 1656 that the Free Church had their new pastor. Pastor Burton was not a university man but a coachsmith. He was saintly enough but not strong physically. As the weeks went by the brothers had to help him more and more. John Bunyan not only kept preaching in the church but often went outside the church in Bedford to evangelize in barns and open fields. He found himself contending with a new sect that called itself the Quakers.

A man named George Fox, who had been in Bedford for a short while, seemed to be the founder of the Quakers. Soon Quakers were popping up everywhere, not holding quiet peaceful meetings, but attending the meetings of other churches and openly challenging their beliefs. John formed a low opinion of this new group. He knew many of these new Quakers from his old wretched days; many of them were former Ranters. The Ranters were so extreme they were being persecuted by Oliver Cromwell's government, so many had fled into the tolerant fold of Quakers.

"In spite of whatever George Fox intended these Quakers to be, I know many of them are very corrupt," John told Mary.

One day in May of 1656, a Quaker named Edward Burrough was preaching in Bedford on High Street near the Market House. John stopped to listen. Burrough had a powerful way with words. He was very persuasive. That made him very dangerous indeed. John was alarmed. To his astonishment he found himself speaking out openly against Burrough. At first, Burrough was contemptuous of John, but when John countered his every argument with an argument of his own from Scripture, Burrough became angry.

"Who is this infernal pest?" exploded Burrough.

John walked home afterwards, scarcely believing how bold he had become. Now Quakers interrupted John's sermons when he evangelized outside his own church. Debating John in public was a humbling venture though. His quick wit and total recall of Scripture thrashed the Quaker dissidents so thoroughly one Quaker finally screamed in exasperation, "Throw away the Scriptures!"

"At last. Your true convictions emerge," declared John triumphantly. "You believe whatever you want to believe, instead of God's word! You're nothing but mystics."

But the Quakers tangled with him again and again. His sermons changed from a fervent appeal to recognize sin to a heated attack on false teachings that he likened to festering sores. He recalled the fiery tracts he had read in Newport Pagnell. That could be another way to counter his critics and attack their false teachings. But could he write well enough?

With Pastor Burton's encouragement he began writing a tract against the Quakers. As he tangled again and again with Quakers his tract got longer and hotter. One day Pastor Burton said to him, "Here is a preface I've written for your tract, Brother Bunyan."

"Preface?" said John in surprise. And he read:

> *This man is not chosen out of an earthly but out of the heavenly university, the Church of Christ. . . . He hath through grace taken three heavenly degrees, to wit, union with Christ, the anointing of the Spirit, and experiences of the temptations of Satan, which do more fit a man*

for that mighty work of preaching the Gospel than all University learning and degrees that can be had. . .(and I have had) experience with many others of this man's soundness in the faith, of his Godly conversation and his ability to preach the Gospel.

"That's most kind of you. But my tract is not finished," said John.

"You must finish it, or who will ever know all your good reasoning against these Ranters?" said Pastor Burton. "Or it will become so lengthy, no one will want to read it."

Mary, who had just given birth to their fourth child, a son they called Johnny instead of John Junior, craved serenity. "Must we wage war on the Quakers?"

"Yes. It is a battle for human souls. The Quakers have drifted away from the Bible into mysticism, like the ancient Gnostics. Jesus was a historical man who died and rose again, Mary. Not a mystical figure who did not experience human death. If that were so, his resurrection would mean nothing."

"The villains!" interrupted blind Mary, now six. "The Bible tells us exactly who Christ was—and *is*."

John finished his tract and titled it "Some Gospel Truths Opened, by that unworthy servant of Christ, John Bunyan of Bedford, by the Grace of God, preacher of the Gospel of His dear Son." He had it printed by none other than his old friend in Newport Pagnell, Matthew Cowley.

"What will people think of a tinker so presumptuous as to write a tract?" John asked. "Or will anyone notice?"

nine

A Glimpse of Heaven

*T*he Quakers read John's fiery tract, soon known just as "Some Gospel Truths Opened." Because of the loud and vitriolic protests of the Quakers themselves, the tract, which might have disappeared into oblivion, became widely known.

"It seems all England is in the streets debating religion these days," said John after one encounter.

He was becoming known throughout the nearly five hundred square miles of Bedfordshire. The common people listened to him, not at all surprised he was a tinker. The rich listened, amazed that this twenty-eight-year-old firebrand was a mere tinker. Some were amused; some were alarmed. The Free Church of Bedford was becoming known as "Bunyan's People." That identification would not have happened if Pastor Burton had been more active himself, but he was in chronic poor health.

By 1657 a tract was issued by Quaker Burrough in response to "Some Gospel Truths Opened." It was a savage attack directed against John Bunyan, who had a "sinful, wicked, devilish nature" and who espoused "damnable doctrines and errors." The attacks on paper and in public only made John more certain of his position. None of the Quakers justified their arguments to John. And he would not ignore their dangerous drift away from the Bible.

Naturally John was soon writing another tract titled, "A

Vindication of the book called Some Gospel Truths
Opened." John's language was not quite as personal as
Burrough's but contained scalding words like "railings"
and "deceit" and phrases like "blind men in a thicket." One
cogent section read:

> *the opinions that are held at this*
> *day by the Quakers are the same*
> *that long ago were held by the*
> *Ranters. Only the Ranters had made*
> *them thread-bare at an ale-house*
> *and the Quakers have set a new*
> *gloss upon them again, by an out-*
> *ward legal holiness. . . .*

John's answer to Burrough was printed that same year of
1657. It too was attacked by Burrough, but John did not
respond this time. He had defended "Some Gospel Truths
Opened" once. That was sufficient. He was very busy
preaching. And by 1658 his small cottage in Bedford
reverberated with sounds of children: precocious Mary,
eight; Betsie, four; Johnny, two; and a new infant, Thomas.
John finally had a chance to publicly honor his father
Thomas. It had taken many years for him to admit his
father had never been a villain at all, but very stable. John
also asked his father for forgiveness. Now he felt that particular sin was buried forever.

John soon realized his wife Mary had a problem. After
Thomas was born she was not getting her strength back. In
fact, although she tried to hide it, she seemed to be failing.
Fear numbed John. He had seen a mother and a sister just
slip away into death. He thought the unthinkable: was Mary
not going to recover? What would he do without Mary?

When she developed a fever, a black dread seized him. Could the unimaginable happen again? No, not again. Not to his sweet wife Mary. But the rose faded from her cheeks. Her skin had never been whiter. Then Mary slipped away. Inside John cried once again, *Are these the fruits of Christianity? Are these the tokens of a blessed man?* Losing Mary seemed unbearable. And yet, he reminded himself, hadn't he once seen inconsolable grieving as a sign of lack of faith? Mary was in paradise, he told himself. If he didn't believe that, his preaching, his very life, was a fraud.

He told his small children, "Mother is in paradise."

"But what is paradise?" asked Betsie, who had never shown the interest in her parents' conversations that blind Mary had. Betsie indulged her sight on pretty baubles. "What does it look like?"

"Look like?" said John numbly.

"Just before you get there, you stop and rest in Beulah Land!" exclaimed Mary.

"Why, of course, Mary is right!" How John admired Mary's extra senses. "In our Holy Bible the book of Isaiah says:

> *Thou shalt no more be termed Forsaken; neither shall thy land any more be termed Desolate: but thou shalt be called. . .Beulah: for the* LORD *delighteth in thee.*

"But what does Beulah mean?" asked Betsie.

"The Lord's land," explained John. "But more than that, as if the Lord is married to the land."

"But I still don't know what it is," complained Betsie.

107

John was forced to imagine Beulah Land. It was easier if he imagined sweet Mary walking there. He said, "Mother is walking on a way there. The air is sweet and pleasant. The land is drenched in greenery. Orchards, vineyards, and gardens open their gates onto the way. Mother asks a gardener, 'Whose goodly vineyards and gardens are these?' And the gardener replies, 'They are the Lord's, planted here for His delight—and the solace of His pilgrims.'"

"Oh, that's exactly right, Father," agreed Mary.

John went on, "I see Mother entering a garden. She eats its delicacies and strolls the Lord's walks and arbors. There is constant singing of birds, flowers springing from the earth—and the cooing of turtledoves. The sun shines night and day."

"But that is only a resting place before paradise!" interrupted Mary.

"Yes, of course," said John uncertainly. He plumbed the depths of the Bible he carried in his head. "Beyond Beulah is the sight of Paradise. Some of its Shining Ones even came to walk in Beulah Land. Loud voices rumble from Paradise: 'See, your salvation comes!'"

"Oh, describe the city," asked Mary.

"Paradise is built of pearls and precious gems," cried John. "The streets are paved with gold. Reflections of sunbeams off the glory of the city overwhelm Mother with desire. She cries out, 'Tell my Beloved, I am coming.'"

"Go on, Father," urged Betsie.

"Mother can scarcely look at Paradise, the pure gold is so dazzlingly bright. Two Shining Ones in golden robes meet her. Their faces are pure light. Gently they question Mother: 'Where are you from?' She answers. Finally the Shining Ones say, 'Come with us.'"

108

"Are they taking her into Paradise?" cried Betsie.

"Not just yet," answered John. "Paradise is on a mighty hill. Even the foundation upon which Paradise is grounded is higher than the clouds. But Mother goes up with ease, because the Shining Ones are holding her arms and her mortal garments remain behind."

"I can see it," said Mary.

John said, "The Shining Ones are saying to Mother, 'Because you believe in the Lord, you will see the Tree of Life and eat its imperishable fruit. You shall be given a robe of celestial light and you will walk and talk every day with the Lord, for all eternity. You will see no sorrow, no sickness, no affliction, no death. These former things have passed away. You are going now to Abraham, Isaac and Jacob, and to the prophets.'"

"Oh, please go on, Father," pleaded Mary.

"Oh, there's more," he reassured her. "As Mother reaches the base of Paradise, a throng of Heavenly Hosts rushes out of the Heavenly Gate to surround her. The two Shining Ones shout to them, 'This is the woman who has loved our Lord when she was in the world, and she has left all for His Holy Name.'"

Mary cried, "The Heavenly Hosts give a great shout too, 'Blessed is she who is invited to the wedding supper of the Lamb!'"

"Yes, of course," said John. "The Lord's trumpeters make Paradise echo with their music. The Heavenly Hosts swarm protectively around Mother. Bells are ringing inside Paradise. Just over the Heavenly Gate Mother sees letters in gold:

Blessed are they who obey his com-
mandments, that they may have the

*right to the Tree of Life, and may go
through the Gate into Paradise.*

"The Shining Ones suddenly cry out to the Gate, 'We call upon the Gatekeepers: Enoch, Moses, and Elijah.' Above the Gate appear these three saints. 'What do you want of Paradise?' they ask. 'This woman left her former place,' cry the Shining Ones, 'for the love she bears to the Lord of this place.' Then Mother hears a cosmic voice from inside the gate boom throughout Paradise, 'Bring me this woman! Open the Gate immediately, so that the righteous may enter, she who keeps faith!'"

"But what does Mother do in Paradise?" asked Betsie.

"She receives comfort for all her toil," answered John with complete conviction, "and joy for all her sorrow. She reaps what she has sown, even to the fruit of her prayers and tears. She is wearing a crown of gold, and sees the Holy One, for there in Paradise the believer shall see Him as He is. She will serve Him continually with praise, and shouting, and thanksgiving. She will enjoy her friends again who have gone before her. Yes, I see her going to her saintly father. And yes, there is her own mother she hardly knew!"

"Go on," said Betsie.

"All the bells in Paradise are ringing again for joy. Mother is transfigured, crowned with glory, and adorned in a garment that makes her shine like the sun. Hovering everywhere are seraphims, cherubims, and creatures too dazzling to recognize. And the whole Heavenly Host cries 'Holy, Holy, Holy is the Lord God Almighty.' And Mother joins them in immortality to gaze upon the Holy One."

The children were so enthralled with John's story he had to insist the Lord wanted them to fulfill their earthly mission first. They accepted that. John was relieved the children seemed more at peace now. But the reality of losing Mary was hard. For many months, even years now, he had been free of his old torment. It was only when he directed his thoughts inward as he did now that the feeling returned.

At Mary's funeral he saw his uncle Edward and aunt Rose for the first time in years. Edward Bunyan was a servant for Sir Oliver Luke, the father of none other than Sir Samuel Luke. Edward invited John to visit him at Copley Wood End, the estate of the Lukes. Two days later he had a carriage come for John. Uncle Edward and Aunt Rose had occasionally mingled with the Bunyans of Elstow, yet had always been silent figures. Now John understood why.

Such wealth at the great estate at Copley Wood End made a commoner cry. John entered the manor with Edward into the bakehouse, which smelled of fresh bread and pies, and learned that the Lukes stored clarets and other wines in great casks in a cellar below. In the kitchen hung aging meats that the rich dined on regularly and the commoners only dreamed of: red deer, partridge, chickens, ducks, pheasants, salmon.

The manor house itself was a series of quadrangles. From the quadrangle that formed the kitchen, bakehouse, and pantries they walked into a quadrangle bustling with servants. In one small room choked with rich garments Edward stopped to check on a cloak being tailored for Sir Oliver. Edward had purchased the fine French scarlet in London for two pounds a yard. It was to be trimmed with one hundred fancy buttons and loops, which Edward had also purchased. The total cost of the cloak was about 30 pounds, roughly three times what John had carried out of the war.

111

"Above the quadrangles are bedrooms," whispered Uncle Edward.

Edward tiptoed toward the front quadrangle. The front was the glory of the house. Besides sumptuous parlors, a dining hall, and a chapel, there was a long gallery. The gallery was rich paneled wood adorned with paintings on one side and tall stone-mullioned windows on the other. There was also a study with a library. John was surprised to see among the hundreds of leather-bound books both Samuel Luke and Oliver Luke, as well as another gentleman. John was even more surprised when Uncle Edward stopped and nudged him in the door.

"With your permission, gentlemen, this is my nephew, John Bunyan."

"John Bunyan?" Sir Samuel Luke looked puzzled. "Your uncle says you were at Newport Pagnell, Bunyan. I don't remember you there. And yet for some reason I do remember you."

"I look like a thousand English yeomen," answered John, remembering only too well his first meeting with Sir Samuel when he was but a thirteen-year-old scamp, battered from a cavalier.

"They say you wrote the tract called 'Some Gospel Truths Opened,'" said the third gentleman abruptly.

"Yes, sire."

"And are you a tinker by trade?"

"Yes, sire."

"Humbug." With that the third gentleman began to question John savagely.

John knew it was a day to hold his fire. He put on his most placid face and calmly parried question after question. Ever since his army days he had been a brisk talker.

He was even less at a loss for words since he had embraced the Scripture. And he now spoke truthfully and with supreme confidence.

At last the third man shook his head. "I would not have believed it. Thank you, Mister Bunyan."

Abruptly Uncle Edward took him away. When they were dining in the servants' quarters John learned the third man was Lord William Russell. And John now knew that Edward had been asked by his masters to bring John to them. They were probably anxious to put to rest this fraud about a simple tinker preaching and writing. He had disappointed them. He was not angry with Edward. What else could Edward have done?

Besides, it gave John a fresh look at wealth. In the war he had destroyed wealth, almost began to pity the wealthy. His feelings based on the dust and rubble of castles were obviously misplaced. The wealthy were still doing very well for themselves.

Whether his "interview" with Lord Russell and the Lukes had anything to do with what happened in the following days John did not know. Probably Edward's masters only reflected a curiosity about the preaching tinker that was sweeping the county of Bedfordshire. It soon became clear many of the wealthy were no longer amused by the precocious tinker of Bedford. Several brought charges against him for preaching in churches around the county, especially to the east near the professors of Cambridge.

"They want me banned, if not worse," mulled John.

So he focused on his new opposition. He began to blister the intolerance of the nobility in his sermons. And he began writing a tract called "A Few Sighs From Hell." It was based on the parable in the book of Luke about the

113

rich man and the beggar Lazarus in the afterlife, the rich one writhing in the torment of hell and the poor one nestled at the side of Abraham in Paradise. It carried the theme of his earliest sermons, that people could not begin the journey to salvation until they realized how wretched and sinful they really were. No one had less a sense of sin than the wealthy and privileged. What English child didn't know the expression "drunk as a lord"? And what commoner did not know what that meant? So John spent many hours in the cottage with the children writing his latest tract. Finally he asked his old friend Gibbs, still a pastor in Newport Pagnell, to read it.

After Gibbs had read it a while he said, "Your images of hell are almost poetry, John. I read here that in hell the sinner is tied to a stake and his flesh pinched off in tiny pieces for years on end. His body is filled with molten lead. He is run through with a red-hot poker. And these are only fleabites of what remains? His suffering exceeds the stars in the sky? The grains of sand on the shore? The drops of water in the seas? I had no idea you could write so picturesquely. It's stunning. I can't believe you wrote it," he concluded tactlessly.

"Nor can I," agreed John.

Pastor Gibbs read more and commented, "You say God's little ones 'are not gentlemen'?" He smiled approvingly. "You say they 'cannot, like Pontius Pilate, speak Hebrew, Greek, and Latin'?" He looked up. "Attacking the professors, Brother Bunyan?"

"They are intolerant and think no one but they can express an opinion."

"Yes, I've noticed," agreed Gibbs. "Here you say the rich 'build houses for their dogs, when the saints must be glad to wander and lodge in dens and caves.' That's a bit strong, isn't it?"

"Read on."

The pastor's face paled as he read on. "You say here the rich 'strut up and down the street . . .hunting and whoring.' My word, Brother Bunyan!"

"No, Pastor Gibbs, my word," joked John. "Read further."

"It says here the rich are 'striving, by hook or by crook . . .by swearing, lying. . .stealing. . .extortion, oppression, forgery, bribery, flattery, or any other way, to get more . . . .' Brother Bunyan!" Gibbs' face was bloodless, as white as snow.

John said, "Let me recall another passage: 'God prepare me to suffer what from the world shall be inflicted on me.'"

"You will suffer. You are going against the tide now, Brother Bunyan."

"I would consider it an honor if you could write the preface," suggested John.

And Pastor Gibbs wrote in the preface that John had "laid forth with the utmost of his strength" and added "I fear that is one reason the archers have shot so sorely at him," referring to vicious attacks on John by the Quakers on paper and in public, and anticipating far worse, now that John had taken on the gentry and the nobility. "I fear for you, John," said Pastor Gibbs. "Thank God Oliver Cromwell allows dissent—even against the privileged."

But within days after John's tract was printed and distributed the news swept the countryside: The great revolutionary Oliver Cromwell was dead!

"Old Ironsides is dead," muttered John.

"Ironsides?" asked daughter Mary, always alert.

"That was Oliver Cromwell's name in battle," explained

115

John, surprised at the surge of emotion it fired. He hadn't uttered that name in a good dozen years. "He was a great fearsome warrior on horseback."

John thought of Cromwell often in the next days. For years Cromwell had ruled England as Lord Protector. What would happen now? Rumors swept England like an early winter storm that September of 1658. Some said the son of the old king would come back to England to rule. Some said Oliver Cromwell's son Richard would rule.

By the end of the year it was clear: Richard Cromwell was the new Lord Protector. But John Bunyan, who got around the countryside as much as any man, sensed a new mood, especially among the nobility. It was resentment toward the Cromwells. The new freedoms were enjoyed too much by the lower classes. The commoners no longer knew their place. And as long as the rule of England was going to be passed down within families why didn't they have a real king? And this became almost a longing for the old Stuart regime that had ended with King Charles.

"Where are the sons of King Charles, Brother Bunyan?" asked a young maiden, Elizabeth.

John was very pleased with this young woman Elizabeth who came every day to the cottage to help with the children. She was bright, respectful, and very devout. He thought of her as a young girl because he had known her since 1650 when she had been no more than eight or nine years old.

"The princes are living in France, I believe."

"And do they have the royal temperament?"

"Certainly, my little dear. You were but a child when Prince Charles and an army of Scots fought against Cromwell. The Royalists were thrashed, but this Prince Charles will try again, I fear. He is just shy of thirty years

116

in age. His father was king at the age of twenty-five."

As the maiden Elizabeth came to the house more and more, John depended on her more and more. The children liked her very much. The youngest squawked loudly when Elizabeth had to leave every evening after supper. Even blind Mary, who was so perceptive about people, who could fathom a soul from a walk or a whisper, had nothing but kind things to say about Elizabeth.

After John's dear wife had been dead a full year he went to talk to his father Thomas privately. Thomas knew exactly why he was there.

"You begin to see the maiden Elizabeth as a woman and you feel terribly guilty," his father volunteered.

"Yes."

"You resented it when I married again, John. You thought it was too soon. But you never realized why I did it. I had to travel near and far as a tinker. You were the oldest child. If you had been reliable I would not have married so soon. But Willie needed a protector."

"In all the years since Mother and Margie died—fifteen years, is it?—I never realized that. Why didn't you tell me?"

"Perhaps you don't remember what you were like. Besides, you had enough problems."

"So you bore the criticism?"

"Most people understood. As people now will understand if you take a wife. You too travel near and far, but for the service of the Lord. With poor Mary blind and Betsie a mere five, they cannot look after the younger ones. They need a mother. The only questions you must ask yourself are: 'Do I truly love the maiden Elizabeth?' and 'Does she truly love me?'"

John gave the maiden Elizabeth much thought. She was

117

so young. Was he too old for her? He was now thirty years old. Elizabeth was eighteen. Thank the Lord she was not young enough to be his daughter. And in twenty years he would be fifty and she thirty-eight. Would anyone think that unusual? Probably not, if he kept his health. There were many men with younger wives. But he was avoiding the larger question: Did he love her?

He thought about her. She looked nothing like Mary. Elizabeth had dark blond hair, not thick but straight and wispy. Her eyes were a cool gray color without sparkle. She was neither delicate nor shapely, only sturdy. But in the most important respect she was like Mary. She was devout, and it was cheery devotion. And she was curious and even tempered. Surely those were the qualities that got him to thinking about marriage in the first place. But did he love her? If he did love her it would have to be a different kind of love than the love which he felt for Mary.

"Surely there are several kinds of love," he murmured aloud that evening after Elizabeth had left. "One does not love a baby as he loves his wife. He does not love Christ the way he loves his mother. He does not love his mother the way he loves his wife. Nor can one love a neighbor the way he loves Christ. So there are different kinds of love. Don't you agree, Mary?"

"Yes, I believe so," she answered.

"Do you love the maiden Elizabeth?"

"Oh, yes. Very much."

"But does that mean you love her more than your dear departed mother?"

"Oh, no. I don't love her the same way I love Mother."

"I too love Elizabeth," said John, and added, "but not the same way I love your mother."

ten

A Resolute Preacher

*T*he next evening after supper John went outside to the cottage with Elizabeth as she prepared to leave for her own home in Bedford. He said, "I'm going to get someone else to watch the children, maiden Elizabeth."

"But what have I done?" she asked, in shock.

"You've pierced my heart. I can't court you if you remain in my cottage. It would be most improper."

"Court me?" she gasped.

"I'll call on your parents later this evening."

So John began to court the maiden Elizabeth. It seemed apparent from the first evening he called on her that she was enraptured. Still, he had to make sure. Preaching gave him a certain authority that could make a young woman blind to flaws. He gave her many an evening to see his every wart and mole. Even though he was at times the most affable of men, rejoicing in God's love, even singing, at other times he was lost in inner thought, apparently cold and unapproachable.

As soon as John found another housekeeper he was more active than ever as an itinerant preacher, traveling east to the environs of Cambridge and south to the environs of London. Many people came out of curiosity to hear a tinker preach, and left never thinking of him as a tinker again.

But some people were not so impressed. A man of learning from Cambridge University sneered, "Since you do not read the Scriptures of the New Testament in their original Greek how do you dare preach the Gospel?"

John asked, "Do you, sir, possess the original scrolls actually written by the apostles and saints of the early church?"

"Of course not. But I have copies. And I believe those copies to be the true word of God."

"I too, sir, have a copy." John brandished his Bible like a sword. "And I believe this also to be the true word of God."

For the first two years John had preached of the necessity of recognizing sin before a person could be saved. The second two years, spurred by Quakers and Ranters, he had preached on false teachings. In his most recent sermons John had been delving more and more into the nature of Christ. On one night in May of 1659 John preached in a barn a few miles from Cambridge. He sermonized from the fourth chapter of First Timothy, at one point accusing the majority of his audience of being unbelievers.

After the sermon a gowned man confronted him imperiously. "I'm Thomas Smith, rector of Gawcat, professor of Arabic and head librarian at Cambridge University. How dare you accuse the majority of us of being unbelievers? Most of us you have never seen before tonight!"

"I have as my authority the Lord, sir," answered John. "The Lord taught us in the parable of the thirteenth chapter of Matthew that there are four kinds of ground the seed falls in, sir. Only one kind bears fruit!"

Thomas Smith began to discredit John in print, hammering on the point that commoners like John were not qualified to preach. John did not respond. He did not have to. His right to preach was defended by another university man,

Henry Denne. Yet another university man, Pastor William Dell, invited John to preach at his church in Yelden.

John did not want to be diverted from delving into the nature of Christ. In the summer of 1659 he published "Doctrine of Law and Grace Unfolded," describing himself as "that poor and contemptible creature John Bunyan of Bedford." This was a book on the two covenants, explaining how Christ put His people under the new covenant of Grace.

In the late fall of 1659 John finally asked the maiden Elizabeth to marry him. When Elizabeth moved into the cottage as John's wife, the four children accepted her without a murmur of resentment. They welcomed her back. They had missed her. Because she had been a child of the Free Church they had always known her. She seemed a big sister to Mary and Betsie.

One winter evening by the fire Elizabeth said to John, "You have not spoken for a long time. Are you in one of your contemplative moods?"

"You doubt it, don't you?" answered John in surprise.

"Yes, this silence is not the same."

"You are right." And he added solemnly, "Woven into God's tapestry is much woe."

"You had best prepare me."

"Oliver Cromwell sowed the seeds to the destruction of his own government. He threw out the Royalists and ruled with a rump Parliament. Then he dissolved them and ruled just as dictatorially as King Charles had before the Civil War. Only Cromwell himself was capable of holding his new government together. His son Richard has tried to revive the rump Parliament, but he has failed as Lord Protector."

"What does it all mean?"

"The old Royalists and even many of old Parliamentar-ians are demanding the restoration of the monarchy. They figure that way they may also restore the full Parliament once again."

"But is that not an improvement, John? Why are you so downcast?"

"Because the new king might not tolerate Nonconformist preachers like me."

"I've never heard you use that word Nonconformist before," said Elizabeth.

"The word is much in the air these days. With the return of the king will be the return of intolerance, I fear."

Days later Richard Cromwell resigned and fled England. By February, 1660, General George Monck had led an army into London to force Richard Cromwell's rump Parliament to dissolve. The common people soon learned that in what was grandly called the Declaration of Breda Prince Charles agreed to accept a parliamentary govern-ment, allow religious freedom, and grant amnesty to his political opponents. By May he returned to England—as King Charles the Second.

John continued to preach as before. Elizabeth told him she was going to have a baby. All the other news was bad. Many changes were made all over the country among mag-istrates, and not surprisingly the new judges were all Royalists. But was Charles the Second going to be a benign king as he promised at Breda? More news drifted out to Bedford like stench from an open grave.

"Why, John, you look white as a sheet," exclaimed Elizabeth one evening.

"News from London. I don't wish to tell you this,

Elizabeth, but you will hear of it anyway, and probably those versions will be worse."

"So I must bear this news whatever it is."

"The new king is arresting everyone who signed the death warrant for his father. They are going to be tried. I fear they are going to be executed."

John's fears came true. Soon all of England knew ten signers of the death warrant were being held for execution. In September Pastor Burton died, followed immediately by the news the Free Church could no longer meet in St. John's. In fact, Parliament had ruled that all pastors ejected after the Civil War were to return to their churches to preach only the liturgy of the Church of England. That day when John had told Elizabeth of the arrests he hadn't been able to bring himself to tell her what else Charles' betrayal of the Declaration of Breda meant.

This is the end of religious tolerance, he told himself.

In their grief for Pastor Burton, and somewhat bewildered, the brothers and sisters of the Free Church set about finding a barn or some other structure where they could hold their meetings. They numbered about two hundred now. Some of the older widows in their flock were those very women who had won John's heart many years before.

In London the ten men from Oliver Cromwell's old government were hanged. That did not satisfy the Royalists. The dead men were drawn and quartered, and their body parts hung about the city. It was reported that the heads of two of them were prominently displayed in Westminster Hall, the very place King Charles the First had been tried. Elizabeth did not want to believe such barbarity, and John said nothing to persuade her. But his memories of the war told him the rumors were only too true.

123

John still preached all over the countryside. One day in November he traveled over ten miles south of Bedford to the village of Lower Samsell. This was a favorite part of the county to John. The low clay plains of his usual surroundings gave way to rolling chalk hills at Harlington, and to the southeast, near Sharpenhoe, the hills were crowned by Clappers Wood. Below that inviting sight was the Houghton House, a particularly fine palace in John's experience.

But the place where he usually preached was an old estate east of Lower Samsell. It was surrounded by huge elms and still had the sunken remnant of a moat. In fair weather John liked to preach outside under the shade of a hawthorn tree. But in stark leafless November he went inside the house.

"I see pain in your faces this day," he said to those already gathered inside the house.

"You mustn't preach today," exclaimed his host. "The magistrate of Harlington, Sir Francis Wingate, has sworn a warrant for your arrest if you preach."

John didn't hesitate. "I'll not dismiss our meeting on that account. Oh, come now. Be of good cheer. Our cause is just. To preach God's word is such a good cause that we shall all be well rewarded for it, even if we suffer for it now." John knew he could not back down. How would the brothers and sisters keep the faith if their pastors would not stand up for Christ?

After others arrived from all around the countryside John began the meeting with a prayer as he always did. But as he began his sermon a man stepped forward to interrupt him.

"I'm the constable, Mister Bunyan. I have a warrant for your arrest."

And as quickly as that John was led away to wait overnight for the magistrate to arrive at his house in Harlington. The next morning John faced the judge, Sir Francis Wingate.

"Why aren't you content to follow your calling of tinker, Bunyan?" said the judge.

"I only instruct and counsel people to forsake their sins and believe in Christ, so they do not perish. I can do that and tinker too, quite well."

"Don't you know it is against the law to preach outside the Church of England?" snarled the judge.

"I did not know of any such new legislation."

The judge looked exasperated. "I find you guilty of breaking the statute against unlawful assembly. . . ."

"That old statute of Queen Elizabeth!" John couldn't believe his ears. "That must be one hundred years old and long buried by Oliver Cromwell."

"No! It is Cromwell who is buried!" Wingate was seething. "I'll break the neck of your Nonconformist church, Bunyan. Can you post bond?"

"And what does the bond compel me to do?"

"To stop preaching."

"I won't stop."

"Then you will go to jail."

Before John was led away by the constable, a Pastor Lindale, who served Wingate, taunted John as if he had just won a great victory. So John realized Lindale was probably the one behind Wingate's persecution. Because John had supposedly committed a crime against the county he was transported to the county jail in Bedford. He felt confident that when he came to trial before another judge, one not prodded into enforcing old statutes by a vengeful man like

Lindale, that he could probably talk his way out of jail.

The county jail in Bedford was a two-story stone building on the northwest corner of High and Silver streets. John passed through a door of three layers of oak. He had gone through it numerous times to preach to prisoners, but now saw for the first time what an impenetrable barrier it was when iron bars secured it. He knew debtors were imprisoned on the second floor in four cells and one day room. On the ground floor were cells and day rooms for felons. John was almost relieved as the jailer led him into a cell on the first floor, because lurking below was a dungeon of two large rooms, one in total darkness. Prisoners slept on a pile of straw in the cells. Usually, four or five men lay on the floor, curled against the cold. Occasionally as many as ten men slept in one cell. During the day they loitered listlessly in the day rooms, or in good weather wandered sluggishly in the courtyard.

John spent his first days getting conveniences from Elizabeth and friends, especially blankets and more clothing. Small fires were occasionally maintained in the day rooms but the cells were always as cold as the outside. And what could have warmed him more than his Bible and writing materials? Rumor among the prisoners encouraged John to think he might even slip out to visit his family once in a while. The jailer was a very kind man to prisoners who gave him no trouble and dropped a penny or two in his palm.

"Don't get too comfortable," warned every prisoner he talked to. "Get yourself to trial as soon as possible. They have nothing on you."

"Is it really that simple?" asked John doubtfully.

Finally one man spoke up. "No. It's not that simple. Your suspicion is correct, friend," said the man, but his voice was kind.

"And how do you know, sir?" asked John.

"I'm a law clerk. On the wrong side of the law this time." He paused. "Do you understand at all how England works under a king, friend Bunyan?"

"Why, as far back as I can remember my family spoke of the king and his court."

"Yes, the king is central to the power that controls England, but there is so much more. The king has a Privy Council and two Secretaries of State. And there is the royal household consisting of the Wardrobe and the Chamber, roughly the royal treasury and the royal supplier. And part of his financial arm is the Exchequer, and as illogical as it sounds, the Exchequer is part of the law courts. It is one of three common law courts. The other two are the King's Bench and the Common Pleas. Besides the common courts there are the Chancery and the Star Chamber. Oh, you mustn't forget, the Privy Council also has some judicial power."

"My head is swimming."

"Being a king—or his subject—is not easy."

"And you haven't even mentioned Parliament."

"No, I haven't. As you know the House of Lords is made up of peers and bishops. The king can increase peerages which means more members of the House of Lords. But it also decreases the power of the church because the number of bishops is fixed."

"And the House of Commons?"

"Oh, they are all landowners too, except for a few rich merchants. Far above the likes of us. They are elected, but as you know the electorate is limited to the landed gentry and men of wealth in most counties. 'People of quality' is

127

the phrase."

"It's so complicated," sighed John.

"It's much more complicated than I've stated so far. If you think there's great agreement among the members of Parliament you are wrong. They too have factions of Royalists and non-Royalists, Church of Englanders and Presbyterians."

"If a man could only understand all that. . . ."

"Oliver Cromwell understood. And such a man exists now."

"A man for the common people like Cromwell?" asked John hopefully.

"No. Lord Clarendon is a Royalist of the first magnitude."

One day there was a commotion among the prisoners. They were flocking to the barred windows—the same ones that allowed them to shout back and forth to their families out on Silver Street any day they wanted. But the commotion this day was not over any families. John joined the gawking prisoners. Off to their left they could see people lined on High Street.

"It's a parade of some kind," said one prisoner.

"They're firing muskets in salute," said another. "It must be a great general."

A Quaker, whom John had come to know well, snorted. "It's no general. Look at that elderly man who is the center of attention. He's wearing a great miter on his head. He's carrying a golden crosier. His purple vestments are magnificent."

"He's a bishop," said John lifelessly. "The old Church of England is back with all its pomp and tyranny."

John came to trial the next Quarterly Session in early January. He was marched over to a building called the

Chapel of Hearne. It was right next to John's old school-house, and he couldn't help thinking what a colossal step it was from one building to the other. Five magistrates sat on the bench that day: Judges Kelynge, Chester, Blundell, Beecher, and Snagg. Rumors around the jail were that they were all Royalists and that the head judge, Kelynge, had been one of the magistrates to condemn the ten Cromwellians in London to death.

The clerk of the court spoke first, "John Bunyan, common laborer, is indicted for devilishly and perniciously abstaining from coming to church to hear divine service, and for being a common upholder of several unlawful meetings, contrary to the laws of our sovereign lord the King. How do you plead to this charge, prisoner?"

John remained calm. "As to the first part I commonly go to the church of God, and am by Grace a member of those people over whom Christ is the head."

Judge Kelynge asked, "But do you go to the parish church?"

"No, sir, I do not. I do not find that commandment in the word of God."

"We are commanded to pray!" snapped Kelynge.

"But not to repeat prayers in the Book of Common Prayer of the parish church. Those are prayers made by other men."

"And how do we know," laughed another judge, "that you do not write out your prayers first and then say them?"

"No sir, I never do," answered John. Suddenly a verse popped into John's head. "Surely you honorable gentlemen remember a verse in the eighth chapter of Romans: 'Likewise the Spirit also helpeth our infirmities: for we know not what we should pray for as we ought: but the

129

Spirit itself maketh intercession for us with groanings which cannot be uttered.' " The judges seemed silenced by John's use of the Bible. John continued, "Yes, we can all say the Lord's Prayer with our mouth, yet how many men in their hearts can say with the Holy Spirit the first two words 'Our Father.' If they are not reborn again the prayer is just babbling."

Judge Kelynge said, "That is the truth."

"Praying ought to be done according to God's word," added John.

"This man is very dangerous to the parish church," said one judge.

"Yes, he shouldn't preach," added Kelynge. "Where do you get the authority?" he asked John.

"From verses in the fourth chapter of First Peter: 'As every man hath received the gift, even so minister the same one to another, as good stewards of the manifold grace of God. If any man speak, let him speak as the oracles of God; if any man minister, let him do it as of the ability which God giveth: that God in all things may be glorified through Jesus Christ, to whom be praise and dominion for ever and ever, Amen.' "

"Wait a minute," cried one judge. "I think he's bluffing. He's making up verses. Clerk, bring me that Bible."

After the judges huddled over the Bible they seemed more exasperated than ever with John. Now even Kelynge looked at John with hostile eyes. He was no longer amused by the precocious tinker. He felt threatened.

Kelynge growled, "You may exercise that gift within the privacy of your family. Otherwise, you may not."

"If it is good in God's eyes to exhort my family," countered John, "then it is good to exhort others."

"I can't combat your Scripture!" shouted Kelynge, thinking John had quoted more Scripture. "Confound you!"

"I am guilty of nothing but praying to God with other people and exhorting them as they exhort me."

Kelynge's face was red. "I'm sending you back to prison, Bunyan. After three months you will be asked if you will submit to attending parish church and abandoning your preaching. If you refuse, you are going to be transported to America! And if you are ever found in England again you will be hanged. That is our verdict, Bunyan!"

Later in the day room, a prisoner speculated, "They're only trying to scare you, Bunyan. Besides, it's clear. All you have to do to get out of this jail is stop preaching."

John went to the law clerk and told him about the proceedings. "Do you believe they are just trying to scare me?"

"I have only this to say: Judge Kelynge was held prisoner at Windsor Castle for eighteen years for supporting the first King Charles."

By the middle of January the jail buzzed with news from London that the king had dissolved the Parliament. Apparently they were not radical enough. Charles the Second was proving to be uncommonly treacherous, even for a king.

"Do you suppose it will be more difficult to get out of jail occasionally?" John asked another prisoner.

"You won't get out now. Besides, that is the least of your worries," said the Quaker, who had overheard his question. "Haven't you heard what else happened in London?"

Then John learned a group of fanatics under Thomas Venner had murdered several people in London. The murderers were caught and soon everyone knew of this group of religious fanatics who wanted to overthrow the

131

government. Every Nonconformist, every Quaker, every Presbyterian who was in prison realized the crown might launch a new wave of repression against religious dissent. And who better to use as examples than those already in prison? After all, they were generally deemed the worst. Why else would they have been the first ones locked up?

"Transportation to America is a real possibility now, Bunyan," said the Quaker in the day room in early February. "They might not give you another chance at all."

John asked, "Which do you prefer, brother: Virginia or New England?"

"The fairer climate is in Virginia, but otherwise it is a foul place, Brother Bunyan. It is the origin of that stinking weed men smoke in pipes. And they say black Africans now work the tobacco plantations as slaves. As you might guess, it is the preferred place for Royalists, not for the likes of us commoners. . . ."

"Then New England is to be preferred. . . ."

"Even there, friend, you must make certain you end up in Rhode Island, for the rest of New England is already under the tyranny of an established church!"

"You make it sound grim," said a third man. "But still, transportation to America may be a blessing. In London they're hanging everybody now. Even Oliver Cromwell."

"Oliver Cromwell!" cried the Quaker in amazement. "He's already dead."

"Nevertheless, the bloodthirsty blokes dug up Oliver Cromwell—him, a corpse of over two years—and hanged him at Charing Cross. His rotting head is displayed in Westminster Hall."

How could the news get any worse? John soon found out. . . .

132

eleven

A Free Prisoner

"*D*ear Elizabeth has lost the baby!" he cried at the news. There was no doubt in his mind Elizabeth had miscarried because he was locked up and she was worried sick. As quickly as he could get the jailer alone he asked to visit his home.

"You're too hot right now, friend Bunyan," said the jailer. "Judge Kelynge is still steaming. And even if you weren't hot, I couldn't let you go because the fanatics in London murdered some people. I couldn't let any dissident out now. Wait a spell."

John had no wish to get the jailer in trouble. Who knew how long he would be in jail and need favors? Didn't the jailer look the other way when John read his Bible in the day room? Didn't he pretend not to hear John preaching to other prisoners? But John's heart ached for Elizabeth.

"Please, God, let little Mary and my stepmother Anne comfort her," prayed John

When the clerk of the court came to see John in the day room the first week of April John knew why he was there. It had been three months since the trial.

The clerk said, "Neighbor Bunyan, how are you doing?"

"Very well, thank you, sir. Blessed be the Lord."

"I've been sent here," said the clerk, "to see if you will submit to the laws of the land and not hold public meetings. If not, at the next Quarterly Session, which is imminent, you will be sent to America. Or worse, you will remain here—under the ground."

"Sir, that old statute that is used to imprison me was made against those who planned evil in their meetings."

"They all say the same, even the fanatics." The clerk smiled sympathetically. "Listen, neighbor, if you feel you've been called to preach, why don't you give your good counsel to one at a time in private?"

"If I do good to one by my counsel, why may I not do good to two? And if to two, why not to four? And so on. . . ."

"On to a hundred, I suppose!" snapped the clerk, exasperated. "How do we know you are doing good? You may be doing bad. That's why only the liturgy of the Church of England is allowed."

"Let this matter be judged by the Scripture," suggested John.

The clerk smelled a trap, remembering how John had overpowered the judges with Scripture during his trial. And he soon left, frustrated that John would not submit. What reasonable man would not agree to get out of prison? "What they say is true, neighbor Bunyan," he shouted over his shoulder at John. "There's none like you in all of England!"

"How did it go, friend Bunyan?" asked the Quaker afterwards.

"I'm still here, friend."

"We may get out of here anyway. I hear Charles will be officially coronated in three weeks. As a gesture of his

134

good will he will release many prisoners. . . ."

"All of whom were never supposed to have been in prison anyway, because of his promise of leniency. . . ."

". . . in the Declaration at Breda," the Quaker added bitterly.

The coronation came and went. Some prisoners were released but not John and the Quaker. All they gained was the suspension of stiffer sentences. John was made to understand his leniency from the king took the form that he was not going to be transported to America or executed. In the meantime he was in limbo.

At times he and the Quaker reminded each other that death was still a possibility too. "Many men have faced that doom in England during our lifetimes," said the Quaker, "even the first King Charles himself. At that moment all one can do is die bravely."

John thought about climbing that ladder, and feeling the thick noose around his neck. "I am determined not to flinch a hair's breadth from death, friend. It is my duty to stand for God's Word, whether He will ever look upon me or not, or save me at the last. I will leap off the scaffold into eternity, sink or swim, come heaven or hell. Oh, Lord Jesus, if You will catch me, do. If not, I still do it in Your name."

With the onset of spring John spent more time in the walled courtyard between the prison and Silver Street. So his routine was now to rise stiffly from his pile of straw, limber up by stretching, and ask permission to go into the courtyard. All winter he had spent the day in the day room, shivering, reading his Bible, probing other prisoners for strategies to get out, counseling, preaching, and only occasionally writing. Now he soaked up golden sunshine and busied himself writing. He would stop occasionally to eat some of his daily food ration, which was no more than a chunk of black bread twice the size of a man's fist. Wolfing down the ration was the act of a newcomer or a fool. A prisoner had to savor tiny morsels all day long. Once in a while Elizabeth would get the jailer to pass on a mug of broth with cabbage or turnips or carrots. Then John feasted. But the rest of the time he wrote.

All his life he had sung the Psalms from a popular songbook by Sternhold and Hopkins. They were sung in churches and in the ranks of marching armies. The poetry of the lyrics was unvaryingly written in quatrains. To John, suddenly inactive as he was, they offered a challenge. And moreover he could create his own story. Ever since he and his sweet Mary had read *The Plain Man's Pathway to Heaven* John had wanted to try to write something similar. It seemed a welcome departure from fiery theological writings. It was not long before his head danced with dialogues. One was between Christ and a sinner:

> *Thy mercy, Lord, I do accept, as mine*
> *Thy grace is free, and that thy word*
> *   does say:*
> *And I will turn to thee another time,*
> *Hereafter, Lord, when 'tis my dying*
> *   day. . . .*
> *I fear not but thy love I shall obtain,*
> *Though I with sin be still in hearty love:*
> *I need not yet forsake my worldly gain,*
> *'Tis grace, not works, that brings to*
> *   heaven above. . . .*

136

John wrote quatrain after quatrain. Finally he showed his work to the Quaker. "Read this and tell me what you think, friend."

"After all the squabbles we Quakers have had with you, friend Bunyan?" But he did read John's poetry and was amused. "I see what you're doing. You should publish this."

"They say it's very difficult to publish anything now. Almost impossible outside of London, Oxford, and Cambridge."

"I know of a man in London who would do it: Francis Smith," said the Quaker.

"Francis Smith? I read some Nonconformist tracts written by Smith himself. Are you sure he's not in prison too?"

"No, I'm not sure."

"And besides I'm in prison myself, friend."

"Surely they will ease up."

But the jailer did not ease up. By the next Quarterly Session in August John was still trying to get his case retried. If only he could get it retried he was sure he could convince the judges he was falsely accused and imprisoned under an old statute. The clerk of the court said he would put it on the judges' docket and asked in a casual way if John planned to fight the indictment. John said he most assuredly would. As the session approached, John realized his hearing was not on the docket.

Suddenly one night during the session the jailer led him out of his cell, and across the day room to a side door. He nudged John out into the inky darkness. Except for special occasions when merchants set candles out along High Street, the streets of Bedford at night had light from the moon or none at all. In minutes John was with his family.

"I was shocked he let me out tonight," he told Elizabeth as he hugged her.

"He probably wanted you to hear my story."

"Your story?"

"Yes, I went into the judges' chamber today as they gathered before the session and confronted them."

"You did?"

"Oh, how I trembled before such powerful men. But I heard this session there was a Judge Matthew Hale, a good man who might listen to a reasonable appeal."

"And did he?"

"No. He was sorry though."

Later in jail John heard about Elizabeth accosting the judges. She had worked them over thoroughly. She had thrashed them. He was so proud of her. Those judges might lose a little sleep over the stubborn Bunyans!

The jailer let John out more and more. John even went to the Free Church a few times. It met secretly now. And the meetings moved around from field to barn to orchard. Finally John took his manuscript to Francis Smith in London. Fortunately, although Smith had been in and out of jail three times that year, he was there to take John's manuscript, titled *Profitable Meditations*. But John had no good fortune when he got back to Bedford. The trip had taken too long. The jailer couldn't keep his absence a secret for the five days he had been gone.

"It will be a good long spell before you venture out again, Bunyan," growled the jailer, angry at John for abusing his privilege.

"Bless you for letting me go as you did," answered John.

The future looked grim. He remembered his family with great nostalgia. Blind Mary was now eleven, no longer a plump child but a beautiful young reed. Betsie was a child of seven, bright, but unlike Mary always acting her age. Johnny was five, roguish looking, with a loyal sidekick in Thomas, three.

Weeks went by. When John wasn't writing or counseling a prisoner he was working now. What he did was tag long laces. It was a good industry in Bedford but few liked to tag the end of the laces. So John tagged them by the tens of thousands. His pay was sent to Elizabeth. He had now been in prison one year.

His second year he carved a flute out of an old chair leg. He had always loved music and dancing and singing. Now he taught himself to play. When other prisoners squawked at his crude notes he went into the far corner of the court-yard to practice. It was not long before they stopped squawking and began to sing along with his merry tunes. God was so kind to John. His gifts seemed endless.

John continued writing. He wrote more theology, as well as polishing his poetry. His sermons in the second-floor day room that was used for a chapel and his writing absorbed him. Somehow he felt blessed. Locking him up was only making his writing better. Even the Quaker admitted it was better.

By 1663 he was writing poetry of a freer nature. He still wrote in quatrains, but he had ventured beyond iambic pentameter, which suited a beat when sung, but thudded monotonously on the ear when read. In a book he would call *Prison Meditations* he wrote of his peculiar freedom in prison:

> *For though men keep my outward man*
> *Within their bolts and bars,*
> *Yet, by the faith of Christ, I can*

139

Mount higher than the stars.

Here dwells good conscience, also
  peace,
Here by my garments white;
Here, though in bonds, I have release
From guilt, which else would bite.

The truth and I, were both here cast
Together, and we do
Lie arm in arm, and so hold fast
Each other: this is true.

But John was never one to leave any doubt how he
regarded his captors. Even his Quaker friend paled slightly as he read:

Good men suffer for God's way
And bad men at them rage. . . .
Here we see also who turns round
Like weathercocks with wind. . . .

The politicians that professed
For base and worldly ends,
Do now appear to us at best
But Machiavellian friends.

Over the next years he wrote five theological books and
two more books of poetry. But the book he was finishing
in 1665—*Grace Abounding*—was the best he had done,
according to the Quaker. It was John's spiritual biography.
It chronicled in detail his five years of torment and even

sketched the years before. It was easy for John to remember Pastor Gifford's counsel: he would not mention his service in the war. The Royalists were now in control. Any mention of the war could tilt a decision by the judges from bad to worse.

"Maybe in the future I can add certain details," he told the Quaker, "that now are as touchy as fevered skin."

"Friend Bunyan, don't you ever get discouraged?"

"I could say the same for you. But we both know what a comfort Christ is. No man in Christ can be enslaved or imprisoned. Being in Christ is being free."

But John knew he was far from perfect. Above all, a commitment to Christ made one aware of his own miserable condition. One had to be brutally honest with God at all times. At the end of *Grace Abounding* John listed seven abominations that still lingered in his heart:

1. An inclining to unbelief.
2. Suddenly to forget the love and mercy that Christ manifests.
3. A leaning to the works of the law.
4. Wanderings and coldness in prayer.
5. To forget to watch what I pray for.
6. Aptness to murmur because I have no more and yet ready to abuse what I have.
7. I can do none of those things which God commands me without my corruptions thrusting themselves in, just as Saint Paul said in Romans 7:21: "I find then a law, that, when I would do good, evil is present with me."

Yet John had to admit these never-ending abominations may have a divine purpose. He tried to list good reasons

for such a paradox:
1. They make me abhor myself.
2. They keep me from trusting my heart.
3. They convince me of the insufficiency of all inherent righteousness.
4. They show me the necessity of flying to Jesus.
5. They press me to pray to God.
6. They show me the need to watch and be sober.
7. They provoke me to pray to God, through Christ, to help me and carry me through the world.

John had a friend take the manuscript to his radical printer, Francis Smith, in London. Smith refused to take it, not from lack of sympathy but from the conviction his shop was going to be raided. A young man named George Larkin printed it. And was a prisoner like John Bunyan to be picky? *Grace Abounding* was poorly laid out by the printer but John was already revising it in his mind. Hopefully Francis Smith could print his revision some day.

When John now went to the barred window to talk to his family on Silver Street, he saw an older family. Blind Mary was now fifteen; Betsie, Johnny, and Thomas were eleven, nine, and seven. The children were fidgety. They had not hugged their father in four years. It must have seemed John had been in prison forever. He avoided touching the bars. Elizabeth told him once it broke her heart to see him clutching the bars so desperately. Elizabeth had aged. She looked older than her twenty-five years. And why wouldn't she? A fatherless family of four had been thrust on her, with two young raucous boys close enough in age to scrap and argue all day long.

"You seem sad, Elizabeth," shouted John from his window a few weeks later in May of 1665.

"Bad news from London, dear," she yelled back.

"Is the war going badly with the Dutch?"

She shrugged her shoulders helplessly. "The plague."

Plague! Who had not heard of the Black Death that had swept the known world a few hundred years before? Ever since, each time the plague broke out, people wondered in terror if history would repeat the disaster. And it seemed almost every year had an outbreak of plague somewhere in England, but usually it claimed only several dozen victims, then mysteriously petered out.

After John's family left, an older prisoner, who had been listening, said, "Being cooped up with others is a very bad situation. If only one jailer or guard or prisoner somehow brings the plague in to us it will sweep the prison like fire."

"What is it?" asked the Quaker, who had the veteran prisoner's knack of sensing any new development though he had just arrived.

"Plague," said John.

"Here in Bedford?"

"Not yet, I pray. It's breaking out in London."

The Quaker said, "I haven't been feeling too well myself," and added, his face ashen, "for several days."

"Relax, friend," said John. "Feeling sick is indeed a symptom, but there are others: headache, nausea, vomiting, and aching joints."

"You're right, neighbor Bunyan," said the older prisoner. "I was in London back in the outbreak of 1636. All of those things do afflict the victim. But the thing that makes it undeniably the plague is the appearance of aching lumps

the size of hen eggs in the groin or armpit or on the neck."
He looked at the Quaker. "What about it, friend?"

"Praise God, I have no such lumps."

The older man sighed. "The Black Death is fast. There is
not much thrashing about. In four days you're gone to the
grave."

"Surely some recover," insisted the Quaker. "With God
anything is possible."

"Some years one out of three will recover," said the older
man. "If you last one week you will recover."

Rumors drifted in of the plague in London. By the middle of June the weekly death toll was over one hundred.
Houses were quarantined, and the door marked with a red
cross. Many added the exclamation: "Lord, have mercy on
us!"

By the end of June the jailer called his thirty prisoners
together in one day room. "Neighbors, the death toll in
London last week surpassed two hundred. Rich people are
fleeing to the countryside. Some will come here. A few
might have the plague. Who am I to know? But I do know
we can't stay bottled up in here waiting for the first case to
break out among us, which will mean we'll probably all
get it."

"Get to the point!" snapped a frightened prisoner.

"You may go to your homes. Naturally I expect you to
keep off the streets and out of sight. You don't want to
come back here, do you? I don't believe I have to warn
neighbor Bunyan to stay away from London this time."

So John and other prisoners went to their homes. A few
prisoners who had no place to go stayed in the jail. But
once the jail thinned out it was not so dangerous anyway.
At home John wrote, tagged laces, and enjoyed his family.

He tutored the children hard, once he realized Johnny and Thomas could barely read. Elizabeth wanted them to go to school but she needed help too. And the boys often skipped school. Once again John felt guilty as he remembered how ungrateful he had been when his father had made sure he went to school.

Plague finally crept into Bedford. Then there was a second case. And more. All deaths in Bedford were north of the River Ouse. Although John feared for his own family, at least south of the river his stepmother and his father, now a hard-used sixty-two, were spared. Victims were buried in a distant field called Pesthouse Close. The aura around Bedford was grim—but news from London was much, much worse.

In late August a visiting friend said, "All shops are closed in London now. There is not one boat on the Thames."

"Surely," said Elizabeth, "it can't be that bad."

The friend said, "The plague is killing poor innocents so fast in London the corpse bearers can no longer work just at night. They are stacking victims in carts and burying them in open fields outside the city."

John sighed. "I'm afraid to ask the death toll."

"Six thousand died in London last week," said the friend.

"Is God taking out his wrath against London for bringing back a king?" asked Betsie.

John said, "The king and his court have fled the wrath. It is the commoners who suffer, dear child. So perhaps the devil is behind it."

It was not until October that the weekly death toll decreased. *Praise the Lord,* thought John, *it has run its wicked course.* By the end of November the weekly toll was three hundred. Such terrible news was now greeted with relief. The end was in sight.

By New Year's Day of 1666 people were returning to London and opening the shops again. Bedford was not untouched, losing forty of its two thousand residents, but London's toll was staggering. In one terrible year London had lost as many people as had been killed in all of England in the long years of the Civil War!

At home John had mixed emotions. "Praise the Lord it is over, but I fear now I must go back to prison."

"I sense a different mood now," said Elizabeth optimistically. "Perhaps the Royalists have had their revenge. Maybe they will let you go in a short while."

"Thank God I had these moments of freedom. The children can now read and write. And of course there is our own great gift from God."

"Yes, that is a miracle," agreed Elizabeth in a very pleased voice.

Prison was different when John returned. In one of the mysterious happenings that a prisoner is never privy to know the why or wherefore, the Quaker was gone. John had wanted to talk to the Quaker, to tell him of his own great gift from God.

So he told the jailer, "Neighbor, my wife Elizabeth is going to have a baby."

"Perhaps you'll be there when the baby is born," encouraged the jailer.

Things were more relaxed in prison now. The jailer was letting the more reliable prisoners slip away in the night. And as hard as John chewed on every crumb of information, like every other prisoner, he still was not prepared for the visit from the clerk of the court.

"Bunyan, you're being paroled."

And John was home that spring when a baby daughter, Sarah, was born.

The Free Church was still meeting secretly, though membership had dwindled to about fifty. For a few weeks John counseled members in private. He had to give Elizabeth time to get her strength back. Certain things had to be done to the cottage. He had to spend time with his children. He had to find out about the status of his books from his printer Francis Smith. But the time came when he had to honor his calling.

When John began giving sermons again, the audience swelled with each succeeding sermon. Soon several hundred would gather under an oak in some distant field or in a hay-littered barn. In a county like Bedford a few hundred people could not gather in secret for very long. And John trembled to think what would happen when they were discovered.

One warm July day as John had just begun his sermon, "Do you believe in the Son of God?" a man trudged forward reluctantly. "John Bunyan?" he grunted.

"Yes. The Lord bless you."

"I am a constable. You are holding an illegal meeting."

Once again John found himself going through the massive oak door of the county prison.

twelve

A Released Pastor

"**B**unyan?" gasped the jailer.

"Yes, friend."

"Good grief, man, why don't you give up your preaching?"

"Why doesn't the king allow religious freedom?"

But in talking to knowledgeable men who traipsed through the prison, John learned of the irony that the king was trying to allow religious freedom. It was Parliament that enforced strict prohibition against religious dissidence. Apparently they felt the king was only advocating freedom so he could champion Catholicism. It was common knowledge his brother James was Catholic in everything but name. And most of the royal family living abroad was Catholic.

"What a twisted, convoluted world we men braid," commented John.

He tagged laces, counseled prisoners, and even gave counsel to outsiders the jailer now let in to consult him. And he wrote. For some time he had wanted to write something pithy and witty like *The Plain Man's Pathway to Heaven*, but in spicy prose with poems sprinkled in for an even greater variety of seasonings. He was hearing from people who had read *Grace Abounding* that they were very pleased with it. He was urged to print more. So he revised it, but it occurred to him maybe his spiritual journey was the proper theme of the larger work that was now always dancing in the back of his mind.

In September of 1666 the prison was once again buzzing with news from London.

"First, the plague, and now, this!" shouted a prisoner breathlessly.

"But how do you know?" asked another.

"The news is all along the Great North Road from London."

"What is it?" asked John.

"A colossal fire in London."

John thought of all the quaint wooden structures nestled together all over London. "A person could run all across London on its rooftops," he muttered.

"And so can a fire," added a prisoner, finishing his thought.

Once again they waited for further news. It flooded in. Whereas the plague took nine months to run its course, the fire ran its course in five days. Once again there was talk of God's wrath.

John only said, "I hope to God that King Charles and Parliament think so. Maybe they'll free their oppressed."

But how could one find any comfort in the news that tens of thousands of Londoners had lost everything but the clothes they wore? As if to tweak John's nose and remind him the bell tolled for him too, he heard all the copies of his books stored in Francis Smith's warehouse had burned!

John had been a very sore point with all magistrates and constables. But even such raw anger grows dull in time. By the fall of 1668 he was drifting in and out of the prison again. He was not rash enough to preach. That would cause him to be tightly controlled again. He had to take what he could get. So he visited members of the church, counseling them on their problems, settling disputes, and instructing invalids.

It was the instruction of the ignorant that got him to thinking about the great work he still had not started. He was writing a tract called, "The Heavenly Footman." It was about a man's foot race to heaven and salvation. It was to be full of obstacles to the man's success: friends pleading with him not to leave them, detours into quagmires, and dead ends. And it was to be full of reasons why other runners failed: acquiescence to professors' lies, clothing weighted down by doubts. And as he began to write, the story grew and grew until it was far larger than "The Heavenly Footman." He put the manuscript aside. His mind was growing an enormous work.

Something else made him receptive to a large work. Getting anything printed now was very difficult. Certain people like John could not be licensed. So what better time to write some *magnum opus* that might take several years? He wanted to create some work so entertaining it could not be put down, but so instructive it could not be forgotten. And finally he thought of expanding the theme of "The Heavenly Footman" into an enormous allegory. He would write a story of a man sensing sin for the first time, and his very complicated and treacherous destiny.

"Make him a pilgrim," suggested Elizabeth.

"On a journey to heaven. . ." mulled John.

"To the Celestial City," cried Mary.

"But with great difficulties," enthused Elizabeth, clapping her hands.

Soon John had finished the first part of his *opus*. It was in the form of a recollection of a man awakening from a dream. The narrator dreams of a man named Christian, who lives in the City of Destruction. After Christian begins to read the Bible he becomes agonizingly aware of the great burden of guilt on his back. For days he wails in the fields. Finally a man called Evangelist spots him and tells him he can rid himself of his burden only by going off to a distant wicket gate. Everyone in Christian's family thinks he is crazy to go. As much as he does not want to leave his family he must go to rid himself of the burden. Neighbors named Obstinate and Pliable try to stop him. He convinces Pliable to go with him. Christian almost sinks in the bog called Slough of Despond, but a man named Help pulls him out. Pliable has already gone back to Destruction. The journey is too difficult.

Before Christian can get to the gate, a man called Worldly Wiseman detours him toward a mountain where the town of Morality lies to get counsel from a man called Legality. Fortunately, Evangelist discovers Christian's error. He sends Christian back toward the wicket gate as the mountain roars words of God: "All who rely on observing the law are under a curse, for it is written: 'Cursed is everyone who does not continue to do everything written in the Book of the Law.' "

"And no one is able to obey every law," explains Evangelist.

Christian hurries on, refusing to speak to anyone. He finds the way again, and in time comes to the wicket gate. Over the small narrow gate is written: "Knock and the door

will be opened to you."
He knocks, crying:

> *May I now enter here?*
> *Will he within*
> *Open to sorry me,*
> *though I have been*
> *An undeserving rebel?*
> *Then shall I not fail to sing*
> *his lasting praise on high.*

A man named Goodwill opens the gate and yanks him inside before the devil can waylay him at the last moment. And that was how far John got Christian on the first part of his *opus*.

John had other prisoners read this first part, which was over 5,000 words. He intentionally picked felons who showed little interest in religion. He asked them to explain what they read. He listened to their questions. He read to prisoners who couldn't read. He asked them to expand on what he read. He listened to their questions. Then he revised. Every truth he asserted was supported by Scripture, and often but not always he would note in the margin the chapter and verse of his source. He had his family read the manuscript too, but the opinions of the prisoners affected his writing more. His family was too familiar with the trip to salvation. He wanted to save those who needed saving. And he worked on each part until the prisoners not only understood it but until it stuck.

His allegory was not simple by any means. His Slough of Despond where Christian had floundered until Help came had many facets. The miry bog could not be improved, even though the Lord would have preferred that. When the sinner finally had a conviction he was a sinner, fears and doubts arose to settle like scum and filth into that depression. For over a thousand years the Lord's helpers tried to improve that bad ground by pouring wagonloads of fill, with millions of instructions, into the slough. They even built steps though the slough, yet fears and doubts overwhelm the sinners and they tumble into the slough anyway.

"When are you going to take it to the printer, neighbor Bunyan?" asked one prisoner who thoroughly approved of the much revised version he read.

"It's the bare beginning of the story," answered John. "The trip to salvation is long and difficult. I expect the final story to be ten times as long as the piece you have read."

"Truly? Why, there will be nothing like it anywhere in England," marveled the man.

"Perhaps that is why God keeps me here in prison, friend. Otherwise, I might not ever find the time to finish it." Many days John did feel that way. Prison had become his office where no one could disturb him!

"You can certainly see a bright side to a very dark thing." The man scowled.

"Come to Christ, man, and no tyrant can make you a prisoner."

John sat through the long days in prison, not wanting the days to pass but actually savoring every second of light. In a preface to his *opus* he was putting to poetry the very process of writing his book:

153

And thus it was: I, writing of the way
And race of saints in this our
  gospel-day,
Fell suddenly into an allegory
About their journey, and the way to
  glory,
In more than twenty things, which I set
  down;
This done, I twenty more had in my
  crown,
And they again began to multiply,
Like sparks that from the coals of fire
  do fly.

Sparks did fly. John plumbed his memory for rivers and mountains and hills, and even armor and fighting. The hills near Sharpenhoe, which he had always admired for their beauty, became his Delectable Mountains. The Houghton House he liked so much became his House Beautiful. The House Beautiful could not be reached without enormous difficulty so John placed it on a precipitous hill called the Hill of Difficulty. It was none other than the Helsby Hill which his dear wife Mary had struggled up on hands and knees as a child, an experience she had described to him in detail.

And he needed many characters. Dozens. And for each one he visualized a real person he had known to make them come alive on paper. Pliable was a real person. Obstinate was a real person. And on and on. John got a peculiar satisfaction casting his real-life nemesis Judge Kelynge as Christian's nemesis Judge Hate-good. Ranters and noblemen and constables and professors and pastors and tradesmen came alive on paper too, some representing the evil side of man and some representing those saved by God's grace.

There were few men not flawed. They bore the names Simple, Sloth, Presumption, Formalist, Hypocrisy, Mistrust, Timorous, Wanton, Discontent, Shame, Talkative, Say-well, No-good, Malice, Fair-speech, Money-love, Ignorance, Vain-confidence, Turnaway, Little-faith, Faint-heart, Guilt, and Atheist. They came from towns like Carnal Policy, Graceless, Deceit, and Turnback.

Dire servants of the devil along the way were hobgoblins, satyrs, dragons, giants, lions, flatterers, and corrupt men. They lived off the way—yes, even some boldly on the way—in places like Deadman's Lane, Despair, Destruction, Danger, By-path Meadow, Vanity Fair, Valley of Humiliation, Valley of the Shadow of Death, and Enchanted Ground.

Yet the Lord's helpers along the way were named Patience, Amity, Shining Ones, Discretion, Prudence, Piety, Charity, Knowledge, Watchful, Sincere, and Experience. The Lord's places on the way were called Salvation and Deliverance and Beulah and Delectable and Caution.

John sprinkled poetry though the book. Even though Christian still has a long journey ahead of him, when he comes to the cross he loses the burden off his back, that unforgiven guilt, now paid for by Christ's blood. After it drops off his back and rolls into a sepulcher he cries:

> *Thus far did I come laden with my sin;*
> *Nor could ought ease the grief that I*

was in,
Till I came hither: What a place is this!
Must here be the beginning of my bliss?
Must here the burden fall from off my
  back?
Must here the strings that bound it to
  me crack?
Blest Cross! Blest Sepulcher! Blessed
  rather be
The Man that there was put to shame
  for me!

Later in the journey, after Christian vanquishes Apollyon, the terrible destroyer in the book of Revelation, he sings:

Great Beelzebub, the captain of this
  fiend,
Designed my ruin; therefore to this end
He sent him harnessed out, and he with
  rage,
That hellish was, did fiercely me
  engage:
But blessed Michael helped me, and I,
By dint of sword, did quickly make him
  fly:
Therefore to him let me give lasting
  praise,
And thank, and bless his holy name
  always.

John toiled on and on with his book. He was awash in

pages of manuscript, always questioning, listening, revising. He now owned John Foxe's *Book of Martyrs*, but his main library was the Bible and the minds of men and women, poor and rich, saints and sinners.

In November 1670 he observed the completion of one decade in prison. He smelled winds of change. He enjoyed more and more freedom as the jailer let him out at night. But always John had to come back. Always he had to refrain from preaching. His last time at home had been a painful reminder of his chains. He had decided to have a talk with Johnny, now fourteen.

"Johnny, have you made any plans for your future?"

The boy scowled. "I'll be a tinker like you and Grandfather," he replied bitterly.

"But you've shown no interest in tinkering."

"This is England, Father. I am either a tinker or a beggar."

"Oh, don't be so melodramatic, Johnny."

"You know one can't step out of his position in life. Look at you."

Thus enlightened, John returned to prison. The writing of his allegory, which he now referred to as *The Pilgrim's Progress*, was slowing down. The new freedom put more demands on his time because he counseled members of the church and tended to his family. Moreover, he began to squabble in print with a man named Edward Fowler.

Fowler was a Latitudinarian, a man who considered himself very rational. He had adapted to the new Church of England quite handily, declaring that "our Christian liberty" allows us to adapt our faith to "the custom of the place we live in" or "by any circumstance convenient." Any one who could not agree with Fowler was "conceited" and

157

"contentious," merely because they exaggerated their own worth.

John Bunyan went after Fowler with fangs bared. He wrote in "Defense of the Doctrine of Justification by Faith" that men such as Fowler were ignorant "persons who, for the love of filthy lucre and the pampering of their idle carcasses, made a shipwreck of their former faith."

Fowler responded tenfold. He wrote that Bunyan was a "dirty creature" full of "scurrilous and vile language," "ignorant fanatic zeal," "insufferable baseness," "hideous nonsense," "insolent pride," and besides all that he was "most hellish and devilish." It so happened that at this time in 1671 people were expecting King Charles to issue the Declaration of Indulgence for religious dissidents. But Fowler begged that John Bunyan be excluded if there ever was such a declaration!

"If friend Fowler only realized how prison focuses its dissidents," commented John. "What a marvelous battle plan we concoct in prison."

In prison with John were many other dissidents. Even his old friend Pastor Gibbs of Newport Pagnell had been behind bars for a while. They used their time well. They counseled each other on what was the most expedient method to launch their churches full speed when they were released.

John worked on that almost full time now.

Apparently if the Indulgence was declared, licenses would be granted for both a pastor and place of worship. So John consulted with members of the Free Church in and out of prison. By late 1671 the tiny membership of only fifty or so in the Free Church had blossomed into a network of churches that covered six counties, with thirty-one designated buildings and twenty-six preachers, including John Bunyan.

"But, John, is such a large organization real or unreal?" asked Elizabeth, studying his grand plan.

"It's very real," he said, and grinned as he pointed at his head, "up here."

"But when does it become really real?" asked Mary.

"Just as soon as the king and Parliament make up their minds. Rumors say new men are now controlling Parliament, and that these men are not strongly supporting the Church of England. So maybe at last the king will issue his Declaration of Indulgence."

On January 21, 1672, John's church, anticipating his freedom, elected him their pastor. It was a godsend. From that day on he and his family could depend on a small stipend to live on.

"What faith they have," cried John. "I'm still officially a prisoner of the county!"

"The king will free you any day now," said Mary. "I have prayed for that every night for eleven years."

Although Parliament refused to change the law sanctioning only the Church of England, on March 15, 1672, the king declared indulgence anyway: Nonconformists could assemble to worship. Catholics could practice their religion privately. And Parliament, now led by men who were not passionate for the Church of England, looked the other way!

In a daze John suspended his narrative of *The Pilgrim's Progress*, about three-fourths finished—with the sentence "So I awoke from my dream." He left prison to walk to his cottage. There was so much to do. By May he applied for the licenses for his grand network of the Free Church. The

Crown seemed to act upon the licenses with the speed of lightning. The very same month the licenses were in John's hands. By August Pastor John Bunyan and the members of his local church had purchased a barn owned by Josias Ruffhead. Just east of the downtown area of Bedford the barn was situated on a strip of land that also supported an orchard.

John took his family to see it. Mary was now twenty-two, Betsie, eighteen, Johnny, sixteen, and Thomas, fourteen. Holding John's hand was the little girl, Sarah, now six. And that was not all. Elizabeth was carrying another child in her womb.

When Thomas saw the barn he cried, "Why, it's in a pit!"

"No." John laughed. "See that rise to the south?"

"That's the motte or hill where Bedford Castle once stood," said Betsie.

"Yes, four hundred years ago. And this pit, as Thomas calls it, was once the moat around the castle."

"It is unusual," commented Elizabeth dryly, "to descend into church."

"But it looks sweeter than a palace to me," answered John. "To think the Free Church has been without a structure for twelve years!"

The barn became known as the "Meeting Barn," and the members were not at all ashamed of its humble origin. Pastor John Bunyan now became a familiar figure in Bedford. He dressed in cold colors as the Puritans did. He wore knee pants with hose and buckled shoes. Over a long-sleeved white shirt he wore a vest. Only on the hottest days did he not wear a six-piece cape. Always he wore a wide-brimmed peaked hat.

Strangers were warned that the large man coming down

160

the street was none other than the "rogue John Bunyan," who had been in prison many years. Broad-shouldered, he was tall enough to menace a stranger. John knew all that, but he also knew that as he neared people they relaxed. There was a great serenity about him.

The "Roundhead" days were long gone. John's reddish brown hair, parted in the middle, came to his shoulders. Like many fair-complected, ruddy-faced men, his mustache was wispy. His face was stern, but his conversation warm and peaceful and so easily peppered with metaphors and clever phrases the most prejudiced person immediately fell into silence to listen.

One of his first surprises out of prison was a gift from his congregation. It could hardly be handed to him in front of the pulpit, so after one service at their Meeting Barn they led him outside, all obviously enjoying his bewilderment.

"What would require such elbow room?" asked John, perplexed.

"It's a horse," cried blind Mary.

"A horse? Where?" John looked around, knowing Mary was rarely wrong.

From behind some trees members led a buckskin horse. John patted it on the neck, then pried back the lips. "It's a young one."

"Just turned two years of age, Pastor Bunyan," said one of the members. "It's a gelding, young enough to carry you near and far for a good many years."

As John led the frisky horse back to the cottage Elizabeth said, "Such a wonderful horse needs a name."

"Oh, describe him to me," cried Mary.

John pondered the huge gelding. "It's taller at the shoulders than the sheriff's horse, and its coat is curried pure

161

gold. Here, Mary, feel its coat."

"It's so warm and powerful," she said, smiling as muscles rippled under her hand.

"Its mane and tail are long and thick and black as midnight. Its eyes are warm and intelligent, so big they drink in all of Bedford in one swallow," bragged John.

"Ironsides!" cried Mary.

"After Oliver Cromwell and his cavalry?" gasped John.

"Long live the common folks of England," said Mary.

"My rebel, Mary," said John in admiration. "Just be careful where you say such things. But we will indeed call this mighty horse 'Ironsides.' "

thirteen

An Acclaimed Author

*J*ohn plunged into his church activities, which included not only pastoring the Bedford church, but attending to the other churches as well. He was almost like a bishop of the Free Church in the six counties. The great buckskin Ironsides carried him over the rough roads like a feather. He preached in Gamlingay to the east in the county of Cambridge. He preached to the south in Ashwell of Hertsford County. He preached in many towns and villages where there was no Free Church. He was well-known now. He preached as far north as Leicester and as far south as London. He was stunned when he first went into London. Because of the fire the quaint wooden city was gone. It had been rebuilt of brick and stone, solid but cold.

Fortunately he was in Bedford for the birth of his third son, Joseph. As Elizabeth recuperated, holding the baby, she said, "Why don't you slow down for a while, John? Finish your great book."

"It will wait."

He knew Elizabeth knew what he was thinking: prison was a very tranquil place to write. Deep in his heart he sensed trouble ahead. Yes, there was a new tolerance for religion—imposed by the king. But these freedoms came and went like the wind. And besides John saw no acceptance for himself in the faces of the noble and powerful

163

around Bedford. He had stung them too many times. They always were relieved when he was behind bars. Now that he was free he was a greater threat to them. And he never knew from what direction they might attack him.

"I'll take advantage of the lull in persecution to revise *Grace Abounding*," he told Elizabeth.

In the revision he mentioned he had been a soldier. He was too cautious to say for which side he had fought. He included his war experience to show God had spared him from death several times and yet the young John Bunyan had felt not the slightest atom of gratitude. That was how deep in sin he had been. His old friend Francis Smith printed the revision of *Grace Abounding* but John held his breath. Francis Smith was always on the brink of being arrested too.

Most of John's energies went into his own church. And much went into recruiting new souls for the flock. Membership climbed to over one hundred. But some members failed him too. They were publicly accused of their sin in church and had to repent. Some would not. A man named Rush was such an unrepentant drunkard John and the membership had to cast him out of the church. And a woman named Witt was cast out for her compulsion to spread vicious gossip.

Once in 1674 in the bitter month of January John was riding Ironsides near the village of Edworth in Bedford County on his way to a meeting at Gamlingay. At Edworth John stopped to talk to an unmarried maid named Agnes Beaumont, who lived with her widowed father, but was at the house of her brother who lived nearby. She was a member of the Free Church at Gamlingay and was planning to go to the meeting. But the roads had become too treacherous to walk.

"Will you take me on your horse, Pastor Bunyan?" she pleaded.

"I fear your father would not like that," he answered curtly, so she would not ask again.

"I'll risk it," she said.

"Please take her, Pastor Bunyan," implored her brother. "Agnes has her heart set on this meeting. It will break her heart not to go. A Mister Wilson was supposed to take her on his horse, but he never showed up."

At last John took her. He broke his own resolution, which was never to be alone with ladies. He was brusque with them for that very reason. He wanted to discourage any interest that could lead to sin, even to the sin of lust. John did not go back to Edworth after the meeting, so Agnes went home with someone else.

The next John even remembered the incident with Agnes Beaumont was when a constable delivered a summons for him to testify at a coroner's inquest! It seemed that after Agnes went home she found out her father had seen her riding with a man on a great buckskin which could only be John Bunyan's mount and in anger he locked her out of the house. She slept in her father's barn. Two days later her father died alone.

"But what is it all about, Agnes?" he asked her before he went inside the courtroom.

"Some one has spread a terrible rumor about us two. The lie is that my father disapproved of our relationship. So you gave me some poison and I poisoned him."

"Whoa!" John felt dizzy. Was this the way he would go back to prison again?

But this was not the day. Agnes' brother cleared both

John and Agnes. He confirmed their father had been very sick before the meeting. And besides, John Bunyan had not wanted to take Agnes, said her brother. He resisted so, he had to be begged before he would agree to take her. Agnes confirmed every word.

The judge had some heated words for the accuser, a lawyer named Farrow, for during the inquest the judge learned Agnes had rejected Farrow's advances at one time. And outside the courtroom Farrow had heated words for a Pastor Lane, who apparently had brought the rumor about John and Agnes to him.

Elizabeth had watched the whole thing. "That was a close call, John."

"Agnes' heartbroken plea that day made me replace caution with foolishness. I'm forty-five years old and still susceptible to all varieties of temptation. She tempted me to be kind, when I knew the appearance of it was wrong."

Later in 1674, Johnny became the first child to leave the nest. He married, rented a cottage in Bedford, and began to make a living with his father's tools. John was very worried about him. He had never joined the church and seemed very unprepared for marriage. In other words, he was almost like John had been at the same age but not quite so bad!

One evening in 1675 when John came back to the cottage, which was situated only about one block north of their church, Mary asked right away, "What is wrong, Father?"

"Good heavens, why did you say that, Mary?" asked Elizabeth.

"There is a heaviness in his steps. A sadness."

"She's right," said John. "Apparently there has been a change in Parliament again. A Lord Danby has gained power. He's a zealot for the Church of England."

166

Within days the word was official: all licenses granted in 1672 to Nonconformist churches and their pastors were immediately revoked. John continued to preach. To the nobility and magistrates he was the chief of troublemakers. He was virtually the first one indicted. No fewer than thirteen justices of the peace signed the charge! He was certainly guilty; the charge was not for holding an unlawful assembly, but merely failure to attend the Church of England service in his parish. John had argued so persuasively in the past that his assemblies were not unlawful—with no less an authority than God's word in the Bible—it seemed these secular authorities did not want to embarrass themselves again with that charge.

John simply refused to answer the summons and kept about his business. And a peculiar thing happened. No one came to arrest him. Did he have powerful friends after all? Did the authorities disagree about his menace to England? Still, the summons hung over his head like the executioner's ax. Twice in the past he had started a service, only to be interrupted by a constable stepping forward to arrest him. If the prospect of being arrested was not bad enough that bleak winter, John was struck another blow: his father died.

Thomas Bunyan was seventy-three. His will left John one shilling: twelve pence, about what a common laborer made in one day. It was no less than John's two half-sisters and half-brother got. His stepmother Anne got the cottage and all the belongings, which were very scant indeed. John knew his father was so poor he was exempted from paying the county tax in his last years.

"Lord, please forgive me," murmured John as he remembered how badly he had treated his father so many years before.

After the funeral Anne murmured in her grief, "It has been so many years from the day the lad Tommy walked through Ellsbury Wood and found three baby ravens in a nest, their feathers white as snow."

"White ravens?" asked John. "But ravens are as black as hard coal."

"These ravens were white. It was one of your father's favorite stories. Surely he told you?"

Had John heard that story long ago in the cottage at Elstow and refused to listen? Once again he felt crushed by guilt. His boyish mind had conjured up a father tinkering idly about the countryside, evilly talking to lonely wives. His real father had crossed through the woods, marveling at God's creations. "Please forgive me, God," prayed John, "and God bless dear Anne and keep her."

Something amazing happened. John became a grandfather. Johnny and his wife now had a baby boy. It was startling the way his father Thomas died and the boy was born: one generation abruptly passing on and another abruptly beginning. Praise the Lord for his blessings. Now Johnny really needed to settle down.

It was not until late 1676 that John was brought to the bar. His "guilt" of not attending Church of England services in his parish was irrefutable. This time he was imprisoned in the town jail. It was a tiny jail located in a tollhouse on the bridge over the River Ouse. The authorities in Bedford had decided John had been too active in the county jail. There were too many prisoners to influence. John could preach a sermon to forty people any time he wanted to, and he often did. And it was too easy to slip in and out of the county jail into the dark Bedford streets. One could not slip away from the tollhouse jail so easily.

There was a long unconcealed walk of one hundred feet just to reach the north end of the bridge. Some powerful people had given John Bunyan a lot of thought.

The bridge was over four hundred years old. John's cell was on the upper floor of the tollhouse. His window looked to the east, to the downstream side of the river. He was soon to discover that a stone stairway descended inside one of the arches of the bridge to a door that opened near the level of the river. But one did not step out into the river's murky waters but a wooded island.

"A most pleasant place to stretch and stroll," John told his new jailer. "God bless you, sir, for this kindness."

Every morning John rose from his straw to stand by the window and soak in the warming rays of dawn. Jail was harder for John now. He had just turned forty-seven. He was not allowed visitors. And he could not see people on the bridge from his window. But *The Pilgrim's Progress* would make the hours fly by. John treated every twist of fate as an opportunity. Now he would finish his work. Surely someone would want to read it someday.

One of his poems he had already written in *The Pilgrim's Progress* said it perfectly:

> *The trials that those men do meet*
> *withal,*
> *That are obedient to the heavenly call,*
> *Are manifold and suited to the flesh,*
> *And come, and come, and come again*
> *afresh;*
> *That now, or sometime else, we by them*
> *may*
> *Be taken, overcome, and cast away.*

169

> *Oh, let the pilgrims, let the pilgrims*
>   *then*
> *Be vigilant, and quit themselves like*
>   *men.*

So he began to write again. After the sentence, "So I awoke from my dream," which he had written over four years previously, he now continued: "And I slept and dreamed again. . . ." The tranquillity of this prison over a river fit the remainder of his book perfectly. His pilgrim Christian had gone through all the obvious conflict. Much of the rest of the way was full of a false sense of security. First the pilgrim was snared by a flatterer and had to be rescued by an angel, who flogged the pilgrim for his carelessness. Then he battled to stay awake through the Enchanted Ground. After that he reached Beulah, God's resting place for pilgrims before they crossed the river of death to enter the Kingdom. He finished the pilgrim's journey with the poem:

> *Now, Reader, I have told my dream to*
>   *thee,*
> *See if thou canst interpret it to me,*
> *Or to thyself, or neighbor; but take*
>   *heed of mis-interpreting; for that,*
>   *instead*
> *Of doing good, will but thyself abuse:*
> *By misinterpreting, evil ensues.*
>
> *Take heed also that thou be not extreme*
> *In playing with the out-side of my*
>   *dream:*

Nor let my figure or similitude
Put thee into a laughter, or a feud:
Leave this for boys and girls; but as for
  thee,
Do thou the substance of my matter see.

Put by the curtains, look within my vail,
Turn up my metaphors, and do not fail;
There, if thou seekest them, such things
  thou'lt find
As will be helpful to an honest mind.

What of my dross thou findest here, be
  bold
To throw away, but yet preserve the
  gold.
What if my gold be wrapped up in ore?
None throws away the apple for the
  core.
But if thou shalt cast all away in vain,
I know not but 'twill make me dream
  again.

John went back into his manuscript to polish earlier sections and add more poems. It was springtime now. Out of his cell window he watched the gentle Ouse glide below him and wrote a poem for Christian's rest by the River of God:

Behold ye, how these crystal streams do
  glide
To comfort pilgrims by the highway side.

> *The meadows green, besides their*
> *fragrant smell, yield dainties for them:*
> *And he that can tell*
> *What pleasant fruit, yea, leaves,*
> *these trees do yield,*
> *Will soon sell all, that he may buy*
> *this field.*

Six months after John was locked up in the tollhouse he finished *The Pilgrim's Progress*. And to his amazement he was free again. Men had appealed to the lord chancellor and posted a bond for him. Once again he joined his family and his church. He was further amazed to see the crackdown on Nonconformists was over. For some reason tolerance was back in vogue. John was tired of the ebb and flow of religious freedom. He didn't want to speculate any more what various political developments meant. Whatever developed—good or bad for him—it all came from the hearts of corrupt opportunistic men. John would preach and write for Christ. If prison awaited, then so be it.

Once again he became a familiar figure in Bedford.

Many found their way to his cottage on St. Cuthbert Street. It was small, no more than twenty feet wide and not much deeper, but cozy with two fireplaces. Above was a loft bedroom with one dormer. On the first floor the large family parlor was to the left. John's small study was off to the right. In the back of the house were two bedrooms and a kitchen. Behind the kitchen was a garden. At the back of the garden were two small buildings: a stable for the horse Ironsides and a workshop, once full of tinkering tools that were now in the young hands of Johnny. The workshop was used mostly by Elizabeth for her gardening.

Visitors seemed always surprised at how few books were on John's shelves in his study. Much of the space there and on his table was taken by manuscripts strewn about, but he also had a small cabinet with nine compartments. The proudest possession of a man who cared very little for possessions was his chair. It even had arms and a cushion. The very poor sat on benches.

Daughter Mary was now twenty-five, Betsie twenty-one, and Thomas seventeen. Sarah and Joseph were nine and three. They all talked of the coming great event: Betsie's marriage to Gilbert Ashley of the village of Goldington, two miles east of Bedford. Gilbert Ashley was a wealthy miller, who owned Castle Mill. He had championed the Free Church, holding services in his house for Pastor Edward Isaac since 1672. Betsie married him in 1677.

John spent his time pastoring and writing theological tracts. Since he had published *Grace Abounding* in 1666, he had written ten tracts on the nature of Christ and the practices of his church.

It was Elizabeth who asked John the obvious. "Why haven't you taken *The Pilgrim's Progress* to the printer?"

"I'm afraid old friend Francis Smith will be arrested and the manuscript disappear."

"Then take it to some other printer."

"But I wanted Francis to print this one. He's so good. . . ."

"And *The Pilgrim's Progress* is so good you want Francis to have the honor of printing it, don't you?"

"Elizabeth, that is so immodest."

"Show me I'm wrong. Take it to another printer."

So John finally journeyed to London with the manuscript. He would get the advice of none other than John Owen. He had met Owen on one of his trips to London in

1673. Owen had once been the vice-chancellor of Oxford and very influential with Oliver Cromwell. He preached in his own Nonconformist church in Moorfields, north of London. Somehow, in spite of his nonconformity, Pastor John Owen remained free, even attending the court of King Charles occasionally. Owen was rumored to have been behind John's release in 1677.

Owen greeted John, "Pastor Bunyan, how can I help you?"

"I have a manuscript of little importance, yet I fear using friend Smith again lest it should disappear."

"Rightly so. Francis Smith is almost shut down anyway."

"I hoped you would recommend a printer."

"Leave your manuscript with me overnight. Once I know the nature of it I can recommend a printer."

John stayed for tea. Owen chatted with John, telling him that there was a strong rumor King Charles was going to dissolve Parliament and call for new elections. Who knew what would happen? Would religious freedom increase or decrease?

"Or will I go to prison or not go to prison?" grumbled John in a tired voice.

When he returned to John Owen the next day, Owen's eyes were red and his face ashen.

fourteen

A Requested Sequel

"*S*it down, Pastor Bunyan," said Owen in his parlor.

"What is it, sir?"

Owen shook his head. "I once told a friend after I heard you preach in London that I would trade all my knowledge for your power in the pulpit."

"That's most kind, sir. . . ."

"But this floored me." He pointed at the manuscript lying on a table. "I stayed up all night reading it." He smiled. "The winds will change in England as they always do—but you will not return to prison, Pastor Bunyan."

"Why?"

"Because this book of yours will make you a national figure that no monarch will dare martyr."

"Surely you exaggerate, sir," said John cautiously.

"You are much too modest and reasonable to accept my speculation. So let history tell us. Take it to Nathaniel Ponder, Pastor Bunyan. Without delay!"

John learned that Nathaniel Ponder also had a Nonconformist background, and like Owen he was protected somewhat by being connected to the nobility. He occasionally went to jail for printing flaming rhetoric but in his case he was always released after paying a fine. The

175

jailer didn't have to change his straw.

Several weeks later when John was in London he stopped by Ponder's shop on Peacock to see the printer's production of his manuscript. He was pleased as he leafed through it, but Ponder was frowning.

The printer said, "I've found some things for correction, friend Bunyan. And others have flooded me with comments. Can you revise it?"

"Is it not well received then?" asked John coolly, trying not to indulge in disappointment for his long-labored creation.

"I can't print copies fast enough. But some minor corrections are necessary. You must stay right here in London and revise it."

John stayed in London to revise it and was subjected to the wildest talk about his book. Gossip said the king's own court talked about it. Was John being cast as a traitor because of the book? What was the danger to him and his family? He went to John Owen to ask him what he thought people were saying about the book.

John Owen only smiled. "There is a new form of literature sweeping Europe, John. It is a book of prose called a novel. A Spaniard named Cervantes started it with a book titled *Don Quixote*. A novel is a story with a plot and characters that represent real people, however much overdrawn. The debate in the court is whether you have written an allegory only or an allegory that is the first great novel of English literature."

"All this talk in London makes my head swim with temptations of earthly glory. I must return to Bedford."

So John returned to Bedford. Outrage swept England that Lord Danby was consorting with the French. For

French cooperation the English Parliament would allow the public practice of Catholicism again. King Charles looked the other way and let the public outcry destroy Lord Danby. Then King Charles dissolved Parliament and called for a new election. But the election was shocking. The Royalists were trounced.

"But does that mean religious freedom is secure for a while, or just the opposite?" questioned John.

On the streets of Bedford John noticed people pointing him out. What was going on? Some new intrigue? Once he looked outside the window of his study and saw a group of citizens standing there staring at his cottage. Enough! He walked into the street.

"I say, neighbors," he said evenly, "what seems to be the problem?"

"Are you not *the* John Bunyan?" said an older man.

" 'The?' What in heaven does that mean?"

"Why, are you *the* Bunyan who wrote *The Pilgrim's Progress?*"

"Do you mean you've read it?"

"Is there anyone who hasn't?" asked the older man, astonished.

Soon John was back in London, revising the book again. Now fifty years old, it seemed he was a man of some note, the victim of double-takes, stares, and stammering praise. It was a form of idolatry, innocent but base and evil too. It made him very uncomfortable.

"If you enjoyed the tale, praise God," he urged. "The glory is all His."

Back at his printer's shop he learned more of what was being said of *The Pilgrim's Progress*.

"There is an uproar, John," said Nathaniel Ponder, "that

Christian's family must be saved too."

"But how can I do that?"

"By revising the book again or adding a sequel."

"Oh, I'll think about it then. There are other things I want to write first."

Now when John preached in London, even on an hour's notice, the congregation overflowed the church. At home he was writing *The Life and Death of Mr. Badman*—the life of a very sinful man—and trying to ignore the adulation. Besides resenting the misguided attention, he had the feeling his future work might suffer. No new work could break out of the glare of *The Pilgrim's Progress*. But he also had to remind himself not to be ungrateful. If *Pilgrim's Progress* became an instrument which led sinners to Christ or stabilized those already making the journey to Christ why should he be such a thin-skinned fool as to resent it?

And so he toiled on his *Mr. Badman*. The character named Badman is bad from start to finish: stealing, cursing, lying, lusting, abusing, cheating, gossiping, and betraying God. And the brute dies in peace, unrepentant.

John Owen praised the book. "A cutting portrait of a sinful man. And what a fine portrayal of English life in a provincial town."

John soon sensed that the praise of Owen and others who read *Mr. Badman* was polite and directed only at the book's merits. More indirectly he learned readers found the book heavy going, complaining of frequent long passages that were sermons. And *Mr. Badman*, with its portrait of evil unpunished in this world, was too frustrating to a righteous person to ever be popular like *The Pilgrim's Progress*.

178

The year 1680 brought problems to John's family. Daughter Mary, now thirty, was in failing health. John's stepmother Anne died. And it was brought to John's attention with some satisfaction by gossips that twenty-four-year-old Johnny was drinking ale, playing cards, and dancing at every opportunity. Pastor John Bunyan was mortified. At the very moment he was publishing *Mr. Badman* his own son was living the book. And yet, hadn't he himself sinned at the age of twenty-four and treated his father Thomas badly? On the other hand, at twenty-four John had been almost ready to follow Christ. He counseled Johnny and prayed that he would change too.

John now wrote *The Holy War*. It was an allegory, but unlike *The Pilgrim's Progress,* it was more abstract. Nonetheless it contained powerful narrative, John was sure. Christ and the devil fought for the possession of a town called Mansoul. The meaning of the allegory was obvious. On another level the allegory described what was happening in England at that very time. King Charles was consolidating power by controlling towns, replacing good citizens with puppets to the crown. *Holy War* came from John's heart; it had to be written. And it was full of military sensations that only a man who had truly faced the armament of an enemy could describe. It seemed as if only yesterday he'd stood on the wall at Leicester, facing doom. He wrote:

> *Let no man then count me a*
> *fable-maker,*
> *Nor make my name or credit a partaker*
> *Of their derision: what is here in view,*
> *Of mine own knowledge, I dare say is*

true.
I saw the Princes' armed men come
  down
By troops, by thousands, to besiege the
  town;
I saw the captains, heard the trumpets
  sound,
And how his forces covered the ground.
Yea, how they set themselves in
  battleray,
I shall remember to my dying day.

I saw the colors waving in the wind,
  and they within to mischief how
  combined
To ruin Mansoul, and to make away
Her primum mobile *without delay.*

I saw the mounts cast up against the
  town,
And how the slings were placed to beat
  it down;
I heard the stones whizzing by mine
  ears;
(What longer kept in mind than got in
  fears?)
I heard them fall, and saw what work
  they had made. . . .

I saw the fights and heard the captains
  shout,

And each battle saw who faced about;
I saw who wounded were, and who
   were slain;
And who, when dead, would come to
   life again.

I heard the cries of those that wounded
   were
(While others fought like men bereft of
   fear),
And while the cry, "Kill, kill," was in
   mine ears,
The gutters ran, not so with blood as
   tears.

Indeed the captains did not always
   fight,
But then they would molest us day and
   night;
Their cry, "Up! fall on, let us take the
   town,"
Kept us from sleeping or from lying
   down.

I was there when the gates were broken
   ope,
And saw how Mansoul then was stript
   of hope;
I saw the captains march into town,
How they fought, and did their foes cut
   down. . . .

Meanwhile the current King Charles had his accomplice the Lord of Aylesbury, who lived in Houghton House, not far from Bedford, quietly stripping Bedford of officials who were not Royalist. It was a new wave of persecution and the most underhanded play for power yet. John had learned much about it, visiting John Owen in London.

"Your name came up in the king's court, friend Bunyan," said Owen. "It's not the first time. But I wish it were in a happier context."

"What happened, sir?"

"The court was interrogating your town recorder Mr. Audrey for the purpose of proving he is a Nonconformist."

"But he is not."

"So he stated. What he said to King Charles in great heat was 'Your majesty, I was an officer under your father's command the entire war of rebellion. When the war was over I was driven out of the kingdom like many Royalists. I am as loyal now as I was then. I have never attended a Nonconformist church. But if the sermons of the Church of England don't improve, and if the sermons of John Bunyan in his Free Church are as exceptional as everyone says, I may attend one yet!'"

By 1684 King Charles had puppet governments in every town in England. Who needed Parliament? Bedford even drafted a new town charter and hosted a great celebration. Two days later, Lord William Russell, the man who had represented Bedford in the Parliament, was beheaded.

But still John remained free. *Perhaps Owen is right,* he thought. The nobility does not want to make me a martyr. He could no longer deny it: *The Pilgrim's Progress* was a success he could never have imagined. He was told it had already been translated into Dutch and French. Apparently it was as popular in Scotland, Ireland, and the American colonies as it was in England. He was pestered everywhere now for a sequel that would save Christian's family. But the thing that made him agree to do it at last was the fact that others were writing sequels to it. They were not allegories that advanced the Gospel, but mere adventure stories written for profit—a motive John despised. What little money he received from sales was simply shared with the Free Church. To make matters worse some began attaching the counterfeit sequel to the real first part of *The Pilgrim's Progress.*

John stated all this in an opening poem to his sequel:

> *'Tis true, some have of late to*
> *counterfeit*
> *My Pilgrim, to their own, my title set;*
> *Yea, others half my name and Title too*
> *Have stitched to their book, to make*
> *them do;*
> *But yet they by their features do declare*
> *Themselves not mine to be, whose e'er*
> *they are.*
> *If any doubted he was proud of the*
> *original he went on:*
> *My Pilgrim's book has traveled sea and*
> *land,*
> *Yet could I never come to understand*
> *That it was slighted or turned out of*
> *door*
> *By nay kingdom, were they rich or poor.*
> *In France and Flanders, where men kill*
> *each other,*

My Pilgrim is esteemed a friend,
  a brother.
In Holland too, 'tis said, as I am told,
My Pilgrim is with some worth more
  than gold.
Highlanders and wild Irish can agree,
My Pilgrim should familiar with them
  be.
'Tis in New England under such
  advance,
Receives there so much loving
  countenance,
As to be trimmed, new-clothed, and
  decked with gems
That it may show its features and its
  limbs,
Yet more, so comely doth my Pilgrim
  walk,
That of him thousands daily sing and
  talk.

He betrayed his uncertainty about its sequel when he finished the opening poem with what seemed half apology and half prayer:

Now may this little book a blessing be
To those that love this little book and
  me:
And may its buyer have no cause to say,
His money is but lost, or thrown away;
Yea, may this second Pilgrim yield that
  fruit

As may with each good Pilgrim's fancy
  suit;
And may it persuade some that go
  astray,
To turn their foot and heart to the right
  way.

So he went to work. He would simply call it Part Two and print it with *The Pilgrim's Progress*. No one else could do that legally. Christian's wife he called Christiana. He wrote that after she lamented Christian's departure she began to feel guilt for the way she had treated him. At that point she has a nightmare of fiends from hell, then a dream of Christian himself in paradise. She awakes and soon has a visitor from the Merciful One. And in this way she learns how to find salvation for herself and her four boys.

Joining the family is a maiden named Mercy. She is more timid than Christiana but possesses a very pure heart. Mercy's only guilt is that she has to leave her family behind. But Christiana convinces Mercy that by going she will encourage her family to follow, just as she and the boys are following Christian. So Mercy sings:

Let the most Blessed be my Guide,
If't be his blessed will,
Unto his gate, into his fold,
Up to his Holy Hill. . . .
And let him gather them of mine,
  that I have left behind. . . .

John would not admit to anyone that practical, bold Christiana, after her change of heart, was a portrait of his

185

wife Elizabeth and that Mercy was the image of his first wife, sweet Mary. He wrote that the six pilgrims left the City of Destruction to retrace Christian's steps. Once inside the narrow wicket gate on the way to salvation they are escorted by a mighty warrior Great-heart. With their invincible guide their journey is not nearly so precarious as Christian's journey had been. All along the way those who help the Lord's pilgrims sing Christian's praise for his bravery.

As in Christian's pilgrimage John peppered Christiana's pilgrimage with poetry, but these poems seemed more to be sung than those he had written earlier. At one point a shepherd boy sings:

> *He that is down, needs fear no fall;*
> *He that is low, no pride.*
> *He that is humble, ever shall*
> *Have God to be his guide.*

> *I am content with what I have,*
> *Little be it or much:*
> *And, Lord, contentment still I crave,*
> *because Thou savest such.*

> *Fullness to such, a burden is,*
> *That go on pilgrimage:*
> *Here little, and hereafter bliss,*
> *Is best from age to age.*

As he did with the first part of *The Pilgrim's Progress* he solicited comments on the manuscript. But he missed the merciless, impolite critiques of prisoners, and their ignorance too. All who read his sequel were too kind, too knowledgeable. Still, he got the impression they liked the poetry. And the character Valiant-for-truth was popular, as well as Great-heart. And of course there was the satisfaction that came with the family's salvation.

"I must take it—as is—to Nathaniel Ponder in London and get back home," he told Elizabeth. "I'm going to write a book with dear Mary." John nodded solemnly toward a back bedroom, where poor blind Mary now wasted away in bed. . . .

fifteen

A Shared Memory

"Yes," admitted Elizabeth sadly, "you must do that with Mary."

"Remember all the poems I wrote for our children over the years?" John brightened. "No one liked them more than Mary. And I'm going to write a book for children with that poetry. Mary will assist me. After all, I'll have to read them to her—every day."

After he had taken his sequel to *The Pilgrim's Progress* to London he returned to Mary to read and discuss the verses:

"A comely sight indeed it is to see
A world of blossoms on an apple-tree.
Yet far more comely would this tree
    appear,
If all its dainty blooms young apples
    were."

"But isn't that exactly what the Lord makes happen, Father?" asked Mary, perking up.

"Why, so he does."
And he read of riders he saw in the country:

"There's one rides very sagely on the

road,
Showing that he affects the gravest
   mode.
Another rides tantivy, or full trot,
To show, much gravity he matters not.
Another claws it up the hill, without
   stop or check,
Another down, as if he'd break his neck.
Now every horse has his especial
   guider,
Then by his going you may know the
   rider."

"And which one are you, Father?" asked Mary, laughing.

"Oh, I'm at our horse Ironsides' disposal and the old plug never likes to go faster than a walk. Another horse in full canter causes him much distress."

"Oh, father, you're joking. Ironsides can run faster than the wind. You walk Ironsides so you can read your Bible."

"Well, the horse must hear it too."

Now with some color in her cheeks, Mary looked like her mother. In fact, she looked older than her mother. John was startled as he realized Mary was now older than her mother had been when she died.

"And what about the drum?" asked Mary and she recited another of their ditties:

"Some horses will, some can't endure
   the drum,
But snort and flounce, if it doth near
   them come.

And John read another:

"The frog by nature is both damp and
cold,
Her mouth is large, her belly much will
hold:
She sits somewhat ascending, loves to
be
Croaking in gardens, though—"

"Unpleasantly!" said Mary, finishing the line. "I don't
wish to ever feel a frog, Father."
John read another, about a snail:

"She goes but softly, but she goeth
sure,
She stumbles not, as stronger
creatures do. . . ."

And Mary continued:

"Her journeys shorter, so she may
endure,
Better than they which do much
further go.
She makes no noise, but stilly seizes
on
The flow'r or herb appointed for
her food,
The which she quietly doth feed upon
While others range, and gaze, and find
no good.
And though she doth but softly go,

190

However 'tis not fast, nor slow but sure;
And certainly they that do travel so,
The prize they aim at, they do procure."

"Now there's a creature that sounds like silk." added Mary dreamily.

"Do you want to touch one?"

"No! Joseph told me they are very pretty to see but cool and slimy to feel."

"Then here's another. Guess which one:

"I spin, I weave, and all to let thee see
Thy best performance but cobwebs be."

Mary blurted the rest of it:

"I am a spider, yet I can possess
The palace of a king."

"And here is something a bit more serious," said John.

"Our Gospel has had here a summer's
  day;
But in the sunshine we, like fools, did
  play.
Or else fall out, and with each other
  wrangle,
And did instead of work not much but
  jangle."

"Well, we're working hard, aren't we, Father? And I

191

shall never forget the Gospel."

"Exactly so. As to the children intended, I say:

> *"I do't to show them how each fingle-*
> *fangle,*
> *On which they doting are, their souls*
> *entangle,*
> *As with a web, a trap, a gin, a snare,*
> *And will destroy them, have they not*
> *a care."*

One morning when John went in to Mary's bed she was not awake or asleep, but in paradise. Of all the children Mary had been the most perceptive, yet the most unable to use her ability in the community. Why did God do such things? Why did some people suffer so much more than others? Or had Mary's life been a thousand times richer than the lives of some with nothing but petty indulgences in their heads?

He remembered lines he wrote for her:

> *Well, Lady, well, God has been good to*
> *thee,*
> *Thou of an outcast, now are made a*
> *Queen. . . .*

Yes, Mary was a queen.

John cried. At last Mary could see the Lord. Maybe she could even see their labor, a wonderful book of poems for children called simply *A Book for Boys and Girls, or Country Rhymes for Children.* How he would miss her!

He was thankful he had spent much of 1685 in quiet

blissful moments with Mary. Now he seemed to wilt.

Elizabeth noticed. "What is next, dear?" She glanced around his study. "There seem to be many manuscripts. Are some of them not published?"

"Just these." He began to paw through the stacks of manuscripts and read the titles. "This: *The Advocateship of Jesus Christ.* And these: *The Water of Life* and *The Jerusalem Sinner Saved,* or *Good News for the Vilest of Men* and *Solomon's Temple Spiritualized* and *Justification by an Imputed Righteousness* and *Paul's Departure and Crown* and *Israel's Hope Encouraged* and *An Exposition on the First Ten Chapters of Genesis.*" And he went on to read the titles of about ten more.

Elizabeth began to wilt herself. "How many did you name? Twenty? But where will you start?"

"I don't know, but I had best get started."

Talking of England was painful for John. Once again disaster loomed. At only fifty-six, King Charles the Second had suddenly died in early February of 1685. King Charles had had no sons, except the illegitimate Duke of Monmouth. Within days Charles' brother James had taken the throne. It seemed to John that each succeeding king was more incompetent. James was certainly the worst in John's lifetime, not surprising since James had never expected to be king. He was unprepared. His abuse of Parliament was nothing new. After all, Bedford's local representative, Lord Russell, had just been beheaded the previous year, and the common folks had hardly batted an eye.

But religion set James apart. In 1672 he had made a public profession of the Catholic faith. Shortly after, he had married Mary Beatrice of Modena, a Catholic. And he was touting tolerance for Nonconformists in their religion, but

193

all the English nobility suspected this really was meant to usher in a tolerance for Catholicism, then a declaration of it as the official religion. It was no surprise that numerous factions began to plot against him. The Duke of Monmouth raised an army against King James that very first summer. Monmouth was defeated, and James decided he had to crack down. Trials so punitive they were being called the "Bloody Assizes" were being held all over England.

"Soon enough they will turn their attention to the Nonconformists," John muttered to himself.

Energy surged through him now. He had no time to waste. John had the titles for all his property changed over to Elizabeth. He worked through his unfinished manuscripts in a frenzy. There seemed not enough time to even stop to eat. The year 1686 brought more changes in the family. Late in the year both twenty-year-old Sarah and twenty-eight-year-old Thomas married. Sarah married William Browne. Thomas took a bride named Frances. Only fourteen-year-old Joseph remained at home. And Elizabeth worried John. She was a mere forty-six, but very worn down. After all, for twelve years she had carried on her brave shoulders a family of four, then five, then six! And the irony of his frenzy of activity was that it worried poor Elizabeth even more.

The year 1687 was no different, with John tirelessly slogging his way though his backlog of manuscripts. As always he pastored the local church, as well as journeyed to the several dozen other churches that he unofficially bishoped. And if that were not enough, he journeyed to London to preach. How could he neglect the place where one of every ten English souls dwelled? In November he had another grandchild. Thomas' wife Frances had given birth to a baby boy, Stephen.

"Too bad I haven't the time to indulge an ancient sentiment," remarked John, "and feel comfortable about growing old."

In June of 1688 the birth of a son to King James electrified England. It was only too obvious there was an heir to the throne now and he was a Catholic. Would England ever stabilize? The nobility and gentry longed openly in the counties distant from London for William of Orange, of all people. William was a thirty-seven-year-old, married to King James' own daughter! Moreover, his father was William the Second, Viceroy of the Netherlands, and his mother was the daughter of Charles the First! So he was son-in-law and cousin and God knew what else to King James!

"What wicked people these monarchs make themselves," summarized John Bunyan. "Their filthy alliances for power are so convoluted one must despair for England."

In August John was asked by a son to come to Reading to arbitrate between himself and his father, who was going to disinherit him. Of course while John was there he had to preach too. In days past when dissenters had been hounded, he had preached there at a house by the River Kennett. The back door faced a bridge which the crowd could use to flee into the night in an instant.

The ride there was over familiar ground. Not only had John ridden old Ironsides there before, but it was the same terrain he had marched over some forty years ago on the way to siege Basing House. John had the strangest feeling this was a last look.

After John preached in a barn at Reading he met the father he had been asked to mollify. The man's face was stone. The son had disobeyed him and the father's heart was just as hard as his face.

"Listen to me, good sir," said John, "to this parable of the Lord's: 'A certain man had two sons: And the younger of them said to his father, Father, give me the portion of goods that falleth to me. And he divided unto them his living. And not many days after the younger son gathered all together, and took his journey into a far country, and there wasted his substance with riotous living.

And when he had spent all, there arose a mighty famine in that land; and he began to be in want. And he went and joined himself to a citizen of that country; and he sent him into his fields to feed swine. And he would fain have filled his belly with the husks that the swine did eat: and no man gave unto him.

And when he came to himself, he said, How many hired servants of my father's have bread enough and to spare, and I perish with hunger! I will arise and go to my father, and will say unto him, Father, I have sinned against heaven, and before thee, And am no more worthy to be called thy son: make me as one of thy hired servants.

And he arose, and came to his father. But when he was yet a great way off, his father saw him, and had compassion, and ran, and fell on his neck, and kissed him.

And the son said unto him, Father, I have sinned against heaven, and in thy sight, and am no more worthy to be called thy son.

But the father said to his servants, Bring forth the best robe, and put it on him; and put a ring on his hand, and shoes on his feet: And bring hither the fatted calf, and kill

196

it; and let us eat, and be merry: For this my son was dead, and is alive again; he was lost, and is found. And they began to be merry.' "

When John left for London, the father and son were reconciled. Even though it was raining, John felt sunny inside from the power of the Gospel. And the secret knowledge that his own son Johnny was shedding his wayward habits and inching toward Christ warmed him too. But by the time he crossed the Thames near Bray he had to hunker down under the shower, now cold and heavy, more like pebbles than rain. . . .

sixteen

A Pilgrim at Home

"Steady, old friend," cooed John in a soothing voice.

He was more concerned about the rain chilling Ironsides, now eighteen years old, than himself. The old buckskin was steady enough on the muddy road, but this was wintry rain for August. And midway to London the rain came down in sheets. To make matters worse John had to ride even more slowly because of the worsening road. The frigid, soggy trip to Snow Hill, near Newgate in London, took ten hours.

John was met by his host John Strudwick, a grocer. "You're soaked clear through, Pastor Bunyan!" cried the grocer.

"God bless you. Please see that my horse gets dry and well fed, Brother Strudwick," said John.

After drying himself and warming by the fire John seemed none the worse for his drenching. His lungs ached from the cold and his head was stuffed up, but the fire revived him. The very next day, August 19, he spoke at Mister Gammon's meeting in the Boar's Head Yard at Whitechapel.

His sermon was on John 1:13, the verse about the children of God: "Which were born, not of blood, nor of the will of the flesh, nor of the will of man, but of God." At one point he pleaded with his congregation, "Look at your neighbor! Do you see a soul who has the image of God in him? Love him. Love him. Say 'This man and I must go to heaven one day.' Serve one another. Do good for one another. And if any wrong you, pray to God to right yourself, and love the brotherhood!" John's sermon that night was pure Christian love. He finished by saying, "Be holy in all manner of your conversation. Consider that the holy God is your Father, and let this obligate you to live like the children of God, so that you may look your Father in the face with comfort on that final day!"

The next day John felt shaky and his head ached. But he had to ride Ironsides to Two Swans by the Bishop's Gate to see his printer, George Larkin. John was pleased the old horse seemed so fit.

Larkin looked at John in astonishment. "Pastor Bunyan? Surely you don't carry another manuscript?"

"Indeed I do, friend. With the quaint title *The Acceptable Sacrifice, or the Excellency of a Broken Heart*, showing the nature, signs, and proper effects of a contrite spirit!"

"Explaining which Scripture, Pastor?"

"Psalm 51. On the verses that say to God, 'For thou desirest not sacrifice; else would I give it: thou delightest not in burnt offering. The sacrifices of God are a broken spirit: a broken and a contrite heart, O God, thou wilt not despise.' "

"Quite so. And you have explained this in how many words?"

"Perhaps not much more than 35,000."

Larkin shook his head. "That's four books this year, Pastor Bunyan."

199

"Is it?" said John nonchalantly.

He couldn't hurt Larkin's feelings by telling him that this year he had also given one book to Nathaniel Ponder and another book to Dorman Newman. And why flabbergast Larkin with the knowledge he still had ten or so unpublished manuscripts in his study at Bedford? And they were not short tracts but books too. Perhaps half a million words!

Larkin frowned. "I fear you're getting run down, Pastor Bunyan. You look very pale today. You should rest."

"Sound advice. I'll go back to Brother Strudwick's and rest straightaway."

John felt worse now. Well, why shouldn't he? He had worked night and day for many months getting his backlog of manuscripts ready. The situation with King James worried him. At his age he wasn't sure he had the endurance to work in prison as he had when he had been younger: writing, preaching, tagging laces. Prison was so cold, so debilitating to the weak and elderly.

By the time he reached Strudwick's grocery, above which were three floors the Strudwicks lived in, he had a fever. He felt very jittery. The grocer looked stricken himself.

John laughed it off. "Oh, it's not the plague, Brother Strudwick. I'll take a nap. But first we must take care of my horse. I'd be a poor master indeed if I didn't do that."

John did not get out of bed that day. The next day he should have felt rested. But he was feverish and ached all over. "Well, it's clear to me now," he told his host. "I have a great cold. What a nuisance I'll be to you for the next week."

"Not at all, Pastor Bunyan."

John was surprised to see a doctor come into the bedroom that afternoon. Strudwick said he wanted to make sure John got the best advice possible. The doctor bled John to combat the fever. Yet the doctor seemed more concerned about John's sweating and labored breathing than the fever.

Breathing was becoming more difficult. And the fever would not break. John began coughing blood. Soon he was exhausted from coughing. His mind drifted. He didn't know if it was night or day. It seemed like a very long time he had been in bed. He ached all over.

Once he looked up to see Strudwick. "What day is it, brother?"

"It's the twenty-ninth."

"Twenty-ninth! Say, I can't lift my head. My voice sounds as wispy as a dead leaf. God in heaven, brother, I believe I'm dying."

"We pray not."

"Oh, don't sorrow. Dying is gain. Life is just a tedious delay of what I expect to be eternal glory." John smiled as he remembered the glory in *The Pilgrim's Progress*. Yes, it would be like that. He was sure. He hadn't made it up. It was in the Bible. God's words, not his.

"Are there things you wish me to do?" asked Strudwick softly.

Accepting his possible end seemed to perk up John. "Oh, my horse. Get the old boy to Bedford, please. He would be miserable without Elizabeth to spoil him with apples."

"What should I convey to Mrs. Bunyan, Pastor?"

"Love to Elizabeth, love to the children. . . ." John's effort was cut off by a coughing fit. He knew now time was short. He recovered enough to wheeze, "I changed all property over to Elizabeth already. Remind her there's

201

forty pounds in my little cabinet in the study—the net worth of the wretched Bedford tinker John Bunyan."

"A mere forty pounds? Why you must have sold thousands and thousands of books."

"Praise the Lord, I have no more money than that."

"Of course, Pastor."

And what of all John's finished but unpublished manuscripts? Suddenly he didn't care. He realized now at this moment of death he would never be through praising God—in this life or beyond. Still, they should be mentioned. "I have some unpublished manuscripts in my study. Do with them as you wish."

"Thank you, Pastor." Strudwick cleared his throat. He looked uncomfortable. "I have a vault at Bunhill Fields. Some right good Nonconformists rest there in Bunhill Fields: John Goodwin and William Jenkyn and John Owen. . . ."

"John Owen? Now there's excellent company."

"Pastor Owen must have had one hundred carriages in his cortege. Yours will be no less. Why, your cortege will assuredly stretch beyond Snow Hill to the Aldersgate and beyond that through the right pleasant fields. . . ."

John cared nothing for earthly honor, but he was too weak to admonish Brother Strudwick. He tried to take a deep breath. He couldn't. He gasped, "Say good-bye to my loved ones for me, Brother Strudwick. Especially sweet Elizabeth."

There seemed nothing else to discuss. Shortness of breath now dragged John from feeble movement into paralysis. He seemed frozen. The fever was gone. It had nothing left to feed on. His mind was clear. It was hard to sense now if he was alive or not, whether he was in his body or aloft. He felt no pain. The room was getting very bright. Brother Strudwick disappeared; it seemed now that he had been gone for some time, maybe days. The room was awash in sunshine. It had to be radiating from a Shining One. Time stopped.

Further Reading on John Bunyan

I. Two bibliographies are particularly useful:

Brown, John, *John Bunyan: His Life, Times and Work.* London: William Isbister Ltd., 1885 (revised numerous times, a more recent edition written by F.M. Harrison, 1928).

Hill, Christopher, *A Tinker and a Poor Man: John Bunyan and His Church, 1628-1688.* New York: Alfred A. Knopf, Inc., 1989. (thematic as well as biographical.)

II. These books by John Bunyan are still readily available. Shown with the original printer and date, all were revised at least once by Bunyan himself.

Bunyan, John, *Grace Abounding to the Chief of Sinners.* London: George Larkin, 1666. (Five revisions by Bunyan. The version edited by R. Sharrock, Oxford, 1962, is heavily annotated and contains Bunyan's "A Relation of My Imprisonment.")

Bunyan, John, *The Holy War.* London: Dorman Newman, 1682.

Bunyan, John, *The Life and Death of Mr. Badman.* London: Nathaniel Ponder, 1680.

Bunyan, John, *The Pilgrim's Progress.* London: Nathaniel Ponder, 1678 and 1684. (There are many revisions and later version of this classic allegory.)

Index